Acts 13-28

"The Church Expands"

#Ac2-NK-SS

A Bible-Based Study
For Leaders and Individuals
Leaders Guide Included

Lamplighters International
St. Louis Park, Minnesota, USA 55416
www.LamplightersUSA.org

FOURTH PRINTING – NOVEMBER 2009

© 2003 by LAMPLIGHTERS INTERNATIONAL. All rights reserved worldwide. International copyright secured. No portion of this book may be reproduced in any form without written permission from Lamplighters International.

All Scripture quotations are from the New King James Version of the Bible. Copyright © 1982 by Thomas Nelson, Inc. Used by permission. All rights reserved.

Lamplighters International is a Christian ministry that publishes Bible-based, Christ-centered discipleship resources. For additional information about Lamplighters resources contact: Lamplighters International. 6301 Wayzata Blvd, Ste 120, St. Louis Park, Minnesota USA 55416 or visit our website at www.LamplightersUSA.org

ISBN # 1-931372-15-2
Order Code Ac2-NK-SS

Contents

How to Use This Study	5
1a/b - The First Missionary Journey Acts 13:1-15:35	7
2a/b - The Second Missionary Journey Acts 15:35-17:15	13
3a/b - The Second Missionary Journey Acts 17:16-18:22	19
4a/b - The Third Missionary Journey Acts 18:23-21:16	25
5a/b - Captured in Jerusalem Acts 21:17-23:22	31
6a/b - Imprisoned at Caesarea Acts 23:23-26:32	37
7a/b - The Journey to Rome Acts 27:1-28:31	43
Leader's Guide	49

4

How to Use This Study

What is Lamplighters?

Lamplighters is a Christ-centered discipleship ministry that is designed to increase your understanding of God's Word and equip you to serve Him more effectively. Each Lamplighters Bible Study is a self-contained unit and an integral part of the entire discipleship ministry.

This study is comprised of five or ten individual lessons, depending on the format you choose. When you have completed the entire study you will have a much greater understanding of a significant portion of God's Word. You will also have learned several new truths that you can apply to your life.

How to Study a Lamplighters Lesson.

A Lamplighters study begins with prayer, your Bible, the weekly lesson, and a sincere desire to learn more about God's Word. The questions are presented in a progressive sequence as you work through the study material. You should not use Bible commentaries or other reference books until you have completed your weekly lesson and met with your weekly group. When you approach the Bible study in this way, you will have the opportunity to personally discover many valuable spiritual truths from the Word of God.

As you prepare for your lesson, find a quiet place to complete your weekly lesson. Each study (Part "a" or "b") will take approximately thirty minutes to complete. If you are new to Lamplighters materials, you should plan to spend more time on the first few lessons. Your weekly personal study time will decrease as you become familiar with the format. Soon you will look forward each week to discovering important life principles in the coming lessons.

You should write your answers in your own words in the space provided within the weekly studies. We have intentionally provided a significant amount of writing space for this purpose. Include appropriate verse references at the end of your carefully worded and thoughtful answers, unless the question calls for a personal opinion. The answers to the questions will be found in the Scripture references at the end of the questions or in the passages listed at the beginning of each study.

"*Do you think*" Questions

Each weekly study has a few "*do you think*" questions. These questions ask you to make personal applications from the Biblical truths you are learning. Make a special effort to answer these questions because they are designed to help you apply God's Word to your life. In the first two lessons the *"do you think"* questions are placed in italic print for easy identification. If you are part of a study group, your insightful answers to these questions could be a great source of spiritual encouragement to others.

Personal Questions

Occasionally you will be asked to respond to personal questions that you should do your best to answer. If you are part of a study group, you will not be asked to share any personal information about yourself. However, be sure to answer these questions for your own benefit because they will help you compare your present level of spiritual maturity to the Biblical principles presented in the lesson.

A Final Word

Throughout this study the masculine pronouns are often used in the generic sense to avoid awkward sentence construction. When the pronouns "he," "him," and "his" are used to refer to the Trinity (God the father, Jesus Christ and the Holy Spirit), they always refer to the masculine gender.

This Lamplighters study is presented after many hours of careful preparation. It is our prayer that it will help you **grow in the grace and knowledge of our Lord and Savior Jesus Christ. To Him be the glory both now and forever. Amen** (2 Pet. 3:18).

About the Author

John Alexander Stewart was born and raised near Winnipeg, Canada. He was drafted by the Pittsburgh Penguins (NHL) and played professional hockey for eight years. He was born again in 1977 when he accepted Jesus Christ alone for eternal life. He graduated from seminary in 1988. He served as a pastor for fifteen years. During this time he planted two Bible-believing churches. He also founded Lamplighters International and now serves as the executive director of the ministry.

Study #1a   The First Missionary Journey

Read - Acts 13:1-15:35; other references as given.

Before you begin, take a minute to ask God to reveal Himself to you through His Word.

1. Jesus Christ commissioned the apostles to be witnesses in Jerusalem, Judea, Samaria, and the remotest part of the earth (Acts 1:8). The first twelve chapters of Acts record the divinely orchestrated "accidental" expansion of the gospel throughout Jerusalem, Judea, and Samaria. Acts 13-28 records the intentional expansion of the gospel from Antioch to Rome, the Gentile capital of the world. **"As they [the church] ministered to the Lord and fasted, the Holy Spirit said, 'Now separate to Me Barnabas and Saul for the work to which I have called them'"** (Acts 13:2). What spiritual qualities were present in the lives of these two men before God called them to missionary work (Acts 13:1-2; cf. Acts 4:35-36; 11:22-26)?

2. The beginning verses of Acts 13 are important because they describe the first planned foreign missionary outreach from a local church. Before this time all evangelistic outreach was carried out by individuals who did not have the specific endorsement of the church (e.g., Philip, Peter). Some Christians go out as independent foreign missionaries without being commissioned by a local church. *Do you think* this is a good idea? Why or why not?

3. Wherever the Word of God is faithfully proclaimed through dedicated servants, God's people can expect Satan to attack the work and workers. Barnabas and Paul landed in Salamis on the eastern end of Cyprus and traveled westward toward Paphos, the seat of government (Acts 13:6-12). In Paphos, a Jewish false prophet named Bar-Jesus (Aramaic for "son of Joshua") attempted to hinder their ministry (Acts 13:8). As an apostle, Paul pronounced divine judgment upon Bar-Jesus because he did not **"cease perverting the straight ways of the Lord"** (Acts 13:10-11). Previously, Stephen prayed for God's mercy for those who were stoning him (cf. Acts 7:60). *Do you think* believers should pray for God's judgment or His mercy upon those who oppose the work of God? Why?

The First Missionary Journey

4. The missionaries left Cyprus and traveled by sea to Perga in Pamphylia (i.e., south central Turkey) where their helper John Mark deserted them (Acts 13:13; cf. 15:38) (Note: Some commentators believe John left because he was not originally called into service by the Holy Spirit.) Paul and Barnabas traveled next to Pisidian Antioch where Paul was invited to give a word of exhortation to those attending the synagogue (v.15). He recounted the history of Israel (vv. 17-23) and said that Jesus was the fulfillment of God's promise to King David that one of his offspring would be the Messiah (v. 23).

   a. Paul mentioned three specific spiritual errors the Jewish people committed during Jesus' life on earth. What were they (Acts 13:26-29)?

   b. What warning did Paul give to the Jews at Pisidian Antioch (Acts 13:40)?

5. Barnabas and Paul were dedicated Christian leaders, handpicked by the Holy Spirit to spread the gospel to the Gentile world.

   a. How did the people respond to Paul's message (Acts 13:42-45, 50)?
   b. Sometimes Christians become discouraged when others do not respond positively to their witness for Christ. How do you normally respond when someone rejects your attempts to witness to them?

6. When the Jews contradicted Paul's preaching, he said, **"It was necessary that the word of God should be spoken to you first; but since you reject it, and judge yourselves unworthy of everlasting life, behold, we turn to the Gentiles"** (Acts 13:46). How do we know that Paul's turning to the Gentiles was God's will and not simply a spiteful reaction to the Jews' opposition?

7. The phrase **"as many as had been appointed to eternal life believed"** (Acts 13:48) seems to endorse a "divine election" view of salvation. However, the next chapter says that Paul and Barnabas **"spoke that a great multitude ... believed."** The latter statement seems to indicate that the speaking ability of the two missionaries was a major factor in the salvation of the people (Acts 14:1).

   a. How can a Christian speak in such a manner that others believe (Acts 14:3; cf. Acts 6:10)?

The First Missionary Journey

b. What kind of things should be absent from a Christian's speech when he shares the truth with others (1 Cor. 2:1-5; Acts 13:10; Titus 1:10:11)?

c. Do you rely on God and His strength or on human ability when you share God's Word with other people?

8. Barnabas and Paul spent a long time in Iconium **"speaking boldly in the Lord"** (Acts 14:3). One would expect great results to occur as a result of the ministry of these two dedicated Christian servants.

   a. What were some of the reactions to their ministry (Acts 14:2, 4, 5)?

   b. How did the missionaries respond to their mistreatment (Acts 14:6-7)?

9. Some Christians rarely witness to others for Christ. Perhaps they have never learned to trust Christ to overcome their fear or they have tried to witness yet believe they have failed. Rather than trusting Christ to help them learn to be an effective witness for Him, they have convinced themselves that they can never become an effective witness for Jesus Christ.

   a. What did Jesus say to the disciples when He originally called them into His service (Mk. 1:17)?

   b. Jesus taught at least two important truths about personal evangelism in this verse. What are they?

Study #1b The First Missionary Journey

> Read - Acts 13:1-15:35; other references as given.

Before you begin, take a minute to ask God to reveal Himself to you through His Word.

10. Barnabas and Paul left Iconium and traveled south to Lystra where Paul healed a man who had been lame from birth (Acts 14:8-10). The healing of the lame man caused the people of Lystra to believe that Paul and Barnabas were the physical manifestation of the Greek mythological gods, Zeus and Hermes (Acts 14:12).

    a. What did Barnabas and Paul say to the people of Lystra to convince them not to worship men (Acts 14:14-18)?

    b. Many people still offer sacrifices to religious leaders in various parts of the world. What do you think pastors and Bible teachers should do to insure that their hearers do not give them undue honor?

    c. Barnabas and Paul told the idolaters of Lystra that God left Himself a witness (Acts 14:17). What was this witness that he left (Acts 14:17)?

11. Some Christians become cynical when they see how fickle people can be. Rather than looking to Jesus for strength, they focus upon the weaknesses of men for whom Christ died. When this happens, they often withdraw or limit their future fellowship with others to casual friendships. As faithful servants of God, Barnabas and Paul respond to the severe treatment they had received from the people of Lystra by simply continuing to do the work that God called them to do (Acts 14:20-22). The two missionaries returned to Antioch, strengthening the believers as they went (Acts 14:21-26). What did they do when they finally returned to the church (Acts 14:27-28)?

12. When Paul and Barnabas returned to the church at Antioch, they gathered the brethren together and reported to the church how God had opened the hearts of the Gentiles to receive the message of salvation.

    a. What specific problem developed in the church during this time (Acts 15:1-2)?

The First Missionary Journey 11

    b.   Paul and Barnabas had great dissension and debate with the religious teachers from Judea who were teaching that a person needed to obey the Old Testament Mosaic Law in order to be saved (Acts 15:2). (Note: Circumcision was the "sign" of the Mosaic covenant which indicated that an individual had fully accepted the Law of Moses.) Why did Paul and Barnabas disagree so vehemently with these religious teachers (Acts 13:38-39)?

13.   When the word *saved* (Gr. *sodzo* - to save, made well, make whole, heal) appears in the New Testament (abbr. NT hereafter), it is often used as a technical term. It refers to the permanent spiritual deliverance that an individual can receive as a free gift from God. When an individual receives this free gift from God, he is safe from all future eternal judgment. In fact, the Greek word, *sodzo*, is derived from an obsolete Greek word, *saoz,* meaning "safe."

    a.   The Bible teaches that Jesus Christ came into this world to save men (Lu. 19:10). It also teaches that He desires all men to be saved (1 Tim. 2:3-4; 2 Pet. 3:8-9). Why do all men need to be saved (Ro. 3:10-13, 19, 23)?

    b.   When a person is genuinely born again, he is given the gift of eternal life. If you died today, do you know for sure that you would go to heaven? (Note: If you are not sure what it means to be "born again" or "saved," ask your Pastor or study leader to explain how you can receive the gift of eternal life.)

14.   Some Christians view their Christian lives as an endless list of spiritual responsibilities that are dutifully executed throughout each day. When a believer has this spiritual perspective, he often fails to experience the joy of God's abiding presence and the thrill of being used by Him in little ways. How did Paul and Barnabas allow God to use them on their journey to Jerusalem (Acts 15:3)?

15.   When Paul and Barnabas arrived in Jerusalem, they were received by the church, the apostles, and the elders (Acts 15:4). The first people to oppose Paul and Barnabas' teaching of salvation by faith in Jesus Christ alone were believers (cf. Acts 15:5). The doctrinal controversy that occurred at Antioch also caused great dissension and debate in Jerusalem (cf. Acts 15:7). How did the Jerusalem church attempt to solve this thorny doctrinal problem (Acts 15:6-7)?

16. The apostle Peter stood up and addressed the other apostles and elders (Acts 15:7-11).

    a. Did Peter's statement to the apostles and elders agree with Paul and Barnabas (i.e., salvation by grace through faith in the work of Christ alone) or with the Pharisees and men of Judea who first went to Antioch (Acts 15:7-11)?

    b. What specific reasons did Peter give to the apostles and elders to convince them that all believing Gentiles should be fully accepted as brethren (Acts 15:7-11)?

    c. What powerful question did Peter ask the spiritual leaders who were assembled in Jerusalem (Acts 15:7-11)?

17. When Peter finished speaking, Paul and Barnabas described the signs and wonders God did through them among the Gentiles (Acts 15:12). After this, James, the half brother of Christ and the leader of the Jerusalem church (cf. Ga. 1:19; 2:9, 12), addressed the assembly and endorsed Peter's (Simeon, v. 14) original ministry to the Gentiles. James gave a final argument that ultimately settled the issue. What was it (Acts 15:15-19)?

18. The combined testimony of Paul, Barnabas, and Peter and the clear teaching of James settled the doctrinal debate. Many years after the beginning of the church, the Gentile believers were finally accepted by the Jewish brethren in Jerusalem. What two things did James recommend to resolve the matter (Acts 15:19-20)?

19. When the doctrinal controversy was resolved among the apostles and elders, the entire church chose two men to return with Paul and Barnabas with the official letter from the apostles and elders (Acts 15:22-23). The letter acknowledged that some of the members of the Jerusalem church had caused a disturbance in the church at Antioch (Acts 15:24). The letter also said that these teachers had gone out on their own without the official endorsement of the apostles and elders (v. 24). Next, the letter endorsed Paul, Barnabas, Silas, and Judas (vv. 25-27). The letter concludes with written confirmation of the church's official position on the issue (vv. 28-29). How was the letter received when the brethren arrived at the church in Antioch (Acts 15:30-31)?

Study #2a   The Second Missionary Journey

Read - Acts 15:36-17:15; other references as given.

Before you begin, take a minute to ask God to reveal Himself to you through His Word.

1. After Paul and Barnabas returned from their first missionary journey, God used them to protect the Antioch church from heresy (cf. Acts 15:1-35). When they had spent considerable time teaching and preaching in the church at Antioch, Paul said to Barnabas, **"Let us now go back and visit our brethren in every city where we have preached the word of the Lord, and see how they are doing"** (Acts 15:36). What happened prior to the second missionary journey that caused Paul and Barnabas to separate from each other (Acts 15:37-39)?

2. Some Bible teachers agree with Paul in his disagreement with Barnabas, with support from the lack of future reference to Barnabas' name in the book of Acts and the church's commissioning of them for missionary service (Acts 15:40). Others say that Barnabas was simply being merciful to John Mark, his cousin (cf. Col. 4:10), who made a single mistake during a difficult situation (cf. Acts 4:36; 11:22-24).

    a. What additional proof does the Bible offer to show that Barnabas' ministry of encouragement was especially effective in John Mark's life (2 Tim. 4:9-11)?

    b. Take a moment to think about a person (Christian or non-Christian) whom God might want you to encourage. List some specific things you could do to encourage this individual.

3. When Paul and Barnabas separated, Paul chose Silas, a prophet and previous leader of the church in Jerusalem, to accompany him on his second missionary journey. They traveled over land through the Roman provinces of Syria and Cilicia, strengthening the churches that had been started on the first missionary journey (Acts 15:41). In Lystra Paul found a young believer named Timothy (Acts 16:1)

The Second Missionary Journey

What spiritual qualities did Timothy possess at this time that made him a good choice for missionary service (Acts 16:1-2; 2 Tim. 3:15)?

4. The financial support of modern foreign missionaries can be an expensive venture that often ends in failure if the missionary candidate never gets to the field of service. What do you think a church should do to determine if a specific missionary candidate will make a good choice for foreign missionary service?

5. Before Paul would allow Timothy to accompany them on the missionary trip, he required Timothy to be circumcised (Acts 16:3). Previously, Paul zealously fought against the Judaizers who taught that individuals needed to be circumcised in order to be saved (cf. Acts 15:1-2). On another occasion, Paul even refused to allow another Christian worker to be circumcised (cf. Gal. 2:1-5).

   a. Why did Paul require Timothy to be circumcised (Acts 16:3; cf. 1 Cor. 9:19-23)?

   b. Paul's action with Timothy (i.e., his desire for him to be circumcised) teaches an important spiritual principle that the church of Jesus Christ has often missed as it attempts to reach the world for God. What do you think it is?

6. Timothy joined Paul and Silas as they continued westward through what is modern day Turkey. When they reached western Asia Minor (i.e., Mysia, Troas), they attempted to go eastward and preach the gospel to the areas in northern Asia Minor that had not yet been evangelized.

   a. A strange event occurred at this time that must have greatly perplexed Paul and his companions. What was it (Acts 16:6-8)?

b. When Paul received the vision from God, he did at least two important things to help him determine if it was God's will for them to go into Europe. What are they (Acts 16:10)?

c. How could you incorporate these two important spiritual principles into your life?

7. Paul and his companions concluded that God had called them to preach the gospel to the people of Macedonia. (Note: This was the beginning of European missions.) During this time Luke joined the three missionaries. The "we" sections throughout the remainder of the book identify Luke's temporary involvement as a member of Paul's missionary band (cf. Acts 16:10-17; 20:5-20; 27:1-28:16). From Troas, the four missionaries sailed across the Aegean Sea (approx. 150 miles) and landed at Neapolis before traveling by land to Philippi.

   a. What was the missionaries' plan to evangelize the people of Philippi (Acts 16:11-13)?

   b. How did God honor their ministry to the people of Philippi (Acts 16:14-15; Ph. 1:1; 4:15-16)?

8. At Philippi the four missionaries encountered a demon-possessed slave-girl who said, **"These men are the servants of the Most High God, who proclaim to us the way of salvation."** (Acts 16:17).

   a. Why do you think Paul did not want this slave-girl to promote their work among the people of Philippi?

   b. Paul cast the demon out of the girl (Acts 16:18). What happened as a result of his action (Acts 16:19-24)?

Study #2b   The Second Missionary Journey

Read - Acts 15:36-17:15; other references as given.

9. Paul and Silas were thrown into prison while Timothy and Luke remained free (Acts 16:24). In prison, their feet were fastened in stocks where they could not easily attend to the bruises they had just received. Instead of complaining or calling on God to judge their enemies, they were praying and singing hymns of praise to God (Acts 16:25). Charles Haddon Spurgeon said, *"Any fool can sing in the day. It is easy to sing when we can read the notes by daylight; but the skillful singer is he who can sing when there is not a ray of light to read by ... Songs in the night come only from God; they are not in the power of men."*

   a. What do you think is meant by the phrase **"songs in the night"** (Job. 35:10; Ps. 42:8)?

   b. Are you experiencing a trial in your life? What could you do to sing **"songs in the night"** and bring more glory to God during your trial?

10. The jailer asked Paul and Silas, **"What must I do to be saved?"** They responded, **"Believe on the Lord Jesus Christ, and you will be saved, you and your household."** (Acts 16:30-31).

    a. What did they mean by this statement?

    b. Some Bible commentators believe Paul and Silas' response to the Philippian jailer endorses "household salvation," a view that children are saved from eternal judgment as a result of the father's or mother's faith (Acts 16:33). Do you agree with this interpretation? Why or why not?

The Second Missionary Journey   17

11. Acts 17 describes Paul's ministry in three major cities and the response of the citizens of these cities to the Word of God. At Thessalonica, the people resisted the Word (vv.1-9); at Berea, they received the Word (vv. 10-15); at Athens, they ridiculed the Word (vv. 16-34).

    a. Luke uses four key words to describe the specific nature of Paul's evangelistic outreach to the people of Thessalonica. Please list these key words and give a brief definition of each (Acts 17:2-3).

    b. What were the results of Paul's careful presentation of the gospel of Jesus Christ (Acts 17:4-5)?

12. The angry mob's accusations of what the missionaries had done wrong is a powerful testimony of the kind of social influence God wants His church to have in every generation.

    a. What did the people of Thessalonica say about the ministry and the message of these missionaries (Acts 17:6-7)?

    b. Could the same things be said in your community about the spiritual influence of the church you attend?

    c. What do you think you could do to increase your spiritual influence on the world?

13. Paul and Silas escaped from Thessalonica at night and traveled to Berea (Acts 17:10). The Bible says the people of Berea were more noble-minded than the people of Thessalonica.

    a. Why was this so (Acts 17:11)?

    b. Do you have a personal Bible study time each day? If not, what are some of the things that hinder you from receiving the Word with great eagerness?

    c. If you are having trouble being consistent in your daily Bible study time, what do you think you could do to be more consistent?

Study #3a   The Second Missionary Journey

> Read - Acts 17:16-18:22; other references as given.

1. On the second missionary journey, Paul, Silas, and Timothy ministered in the churches of Asia Minor until they came to the western coast where Luke joined them. After Paul received a vision from God instructing him to preach the gospel in Europe, the four missionaries entered Macedonia and ministered in the cities of Philippi, Berea, and Thessalonica (Acts 16:12-17:13). In Thessalonica, the hostile Jews incited the people against the missionaries, but Paul escaped and was taken to Athens (Acts 17:15).

   a. Even though the glory of ancient Greece had reached its zenith in the fifth and fourth centuries BC, Athens was still a vital cultural center with a world-famous university. Paul, having been educated in the prestigious university center of Tarsus, must have been excited about the opportunity to visit Athens. What did Paul see in Athens while he waited for the other missionaries (Acts 17:16; cf. 1 Cor. 10:19-20)?

   b. The late Noel O. Lyons of the Greater Europe Mission said, *"Europe is looked over by millions of visitors and is overlooked by millions of Christians"*. How did Paul respond, both emotionally and physically, to the things that he saw (Acts 17:16-18)?

2. Many of the famous buildings of Athens had been built during the days of Pericles (461-429 BC) and were still standing during Paul's visit five hundred years later. (Note: Remains of many of these buildings can still be seen today.) Instead of focusing on the physical beauty of Athens, Paul saw a city full of idols and responded by ministering as God directed him. Today, many Christians see the moral demise of their communities (e.g., gangs, murder, rape, drugs, etc.) but they often do very little to stem the tide of social disintegration. What do you think the church of Jesus Christ can or should do to solve the social and moral decay within our communities?

3. Some of the Epicurean and Stoic philosophers were conversing with him (i.e., Paul) as he reasoned in the marketplace (Gr. agora) everyday with those who happened to be present (Acts 17:18). The Epicureans were followers of the Greek philosopher Epicurus (341-270 BC) who believed that the chief aim of man was pleasure and happiness. Their chief aim was realized by avoiding excesses, the fear of death, and pain. They were existentialists who sought tranquility through personal experience rather than through reason. They believed that if gods exist they do not become involved with human events. What manifestations of this secular philosophy do you see in our society today?

4. The Stoics were followers of the philosopher Zeno (320-250 BC) and got their name from the painted colonnade or porch (Gr. *stoa poikile*) surrounding the marketplace under which he had originally taught his students. They were pantheistic in their theological perspective, believing that all was god. They also believed that life offered both good and bad; the good was to be received without undue exultation and the bad was to be endured with resilient self-determination. They commended suicide as an honorable means of escape from a life that could no longer be sustained with dignity. What manifestations of this secular philosophy do you see in our society today?

5. The Epicureans said, "Enjoy life!" and the Stoics said "Endure life!" Both groups were equally unimpressed with the teachings of Paul. In their question, **"What does this babbler want to say?"** (Acts 17:18), the word *babbler* (Gr. *spermologos* - a seed picker) originally referred to someone who picked up scraps in the marketplace. Later, the phrase referred to someone who picked up various scraps of learning from others and offered them to anyone who would listen.

   a. How did Paul respond to this critical comment (Acts 17:18-20)?

b. How could you apply Paul's example to various situations in life when non-Christians make critical comments to you about the things of God?

6. The Athenian philosophers took Paul to the Areopagus (Gr. *Areiou Pagou* - Hill of Ares; Lat. equivalent - Mars Hill) where he was invited to address those in attendance and present his "philosophy" (Acts 17:19-21).

   a. Many Christians have a difficult time sharing their faith with non-Christians because they do not know how to introduce the subject of spiritual things. Paul's introductory statement to the Athenians reveals an important spiritual insight that can help every Christian become more effective in personal evangelism. What is it (Acts 17:22-23)?

   b. How could you use this spiritual insight from Paul's life to become a more effective witness for Jesus Christ in your neighborhood, workplace, or through your local church?

7. Many modern Bible scholars believe that America has entered the Post-Modern Era. By this they mean that America has now passed the time when society adheres to an absolute standard of right and wrong as revealed in God's Word. Like the philosophers of ancient Greece, truth to the Post-modernist is not determined by some external ethical code such as the Ten Commandments but by one's own concept of truth. According to the Post-modernist, abortion, euthanasia, and immorality are right because they are right for him. When this philosophy is adopted by a nation, it will lead eventually into idolatry and political servitude. What differences do you notice between Peter's message to the religious Jews in Jerusalem at Pentecost and Paul's message to the secular philosophers at Athens (Acts 2:14-36, 17:22-31)?

Study #3b   The Second Missionary Journey

> Read - Acts 17:16-18:22; other references as given.

8. According to some Bible teachers, Christians need to change their approach to witnessing in the Post-modern culture. Rather than initially talking about God (His being, His nature, His righteousness) and man's need for salvation, they recommend a more philosophical approach. Take a few minutes to examine Paul's message to the Athenians. Does Paul take a philosophical approach in his witness to these secular philosophers or does his message emphasize the same elements as Peter's message to the religious Jews at Jerusalem (Acts 17:24-29)? Support your answer.

9. Why is the loving preaching of the gospel of Jesus Christ always God's unchangeable message of hope (1 Cor. 1:21-25)?

10. When a believer witnesses to another person, secular or religious, he can be assured that God is already at work in that person's life. What three additional things can every Christian be assured of when he witnesses to another person (Ecc. 3:11; Jn. 12:32; Ro. 2:14-15)?

11. The apostle Paul told the Athenians that God is the Creator and Lord (Acts 17:24), He is Provider (v. 25), and He is Ruler (vv. 26-29).

    a. What did Paul mean when he said God overlooked the times of man's ignorance (v. 30)?

The Second Missionary Journey

    b.   Why do all men need to repent (Acts 17:30-31; Lu. 13:3; Acts 4:12)?

    c.   What was the Athenians' reaction to Paul's message (Acts 17:32-34)?

12. When Silas, Timothy, and Luke did not join him in Athens, Paul went alone to Corinth. Although Athens and Corinth were only fifty miles apart, the two cities were quite different. Athens was known for culture and philosophy, Corinth for corruption and prostitution.

    a.   What was Paul's emotional state when he entered Corinth for the first time (1 Cor. 2:1-5)?

    b.   Like all people, God's people experience the full spectrum of emotional change. Many times believers are tempted to turn to secular means to alleviate these negative feelings such as fear, anxiety, etc. What did Paul do when he was fearful to the point of trembling (1 Cor. 2:1-4)?

13. List several things that God did to honor Paul's willingness to trust Him when he was tempted to give in to his emotions (Acts 18:1-5)?

14. When Silas and Timothy finally arrived from Macedonia, Paul devoted himself entirely to the Word (Acts 18:5). What do you think Paul meant when he said to

the Jews, **"Your blood be upon your own heads; I am clean. From now on I will go to the Gentiles,"** especially since he had already said that he and Barnabas were turning to the Gentiles on the first missionary journey (Acts 18:6; cf. Acts 13:46)?

15. a. What did God do to encourage Paul during this time of exhausting travel, persecution, ridicule, and meager spiritual results (Acts 18:7-10)?

    b. Think of a time when you really needed encouragement. What did God do to encourage you during this period in your life?

16. Sometimes God's people develop a negative attitude toward the government God placed over them. Rather than being thankful for civil government despite a disapproval of certain legislative decisions, they develop an adversarial attitude toward it. Some believers even refuse to pay their taxes in direct violation to God's Word (cf. Ro. 13:7). How did God use civil government to protect the life of the apostle Paul (Acts 18:12-16)?

Study #4a   The Third Missionary Journey

> Read - Acts 18:23-21:16; other references as given.

1. The second missionary journey ended when Paul went up (to Jerusalem) to greet the brethren and then returned to the church at Antioch (Acts 18:22). After he had spent some time at Antioch, **"He departed and went over the region of Galatia and Phrygia in order, strengthening all the disciples"** (Acts 18:23). Prior to Paul's arrival in Ephesus on his third missionary journey, a preacher named Apollos came to the city (Acts 18:14, 19:1). God had used two lay believers named Aquila and Priscilla to minister and help this man. How did God use them in Apollos' life (Acts 18:26)?

2. It appears that Apollos humbly received Aquila and Priscilla's instruction and continued to serve God. Sometime later, Apollos left Ephesus and traveled across the Aegean Sea to Achaia. (Note: The Roman province of Achaia encompassed the entire Pelopennesian Peninsula, including the city of Corinth.)

   a. God used the apostle Paul to start the church at Corinth during his second missionary journey. Now God directed Apollos to continue the work at Corinth (cf. Acts 19:1). How did Paul later describe their combined efforts to the Corinthians (1 Cor. 3:6, 8-9)?

   b. How did the Corinthian (i.e., Achaia) believers respond to the joint ministry of Paul and Apollos (Acts 18:27-28; 1 Cor. 1:10-15)?

   c. If you are a Christian, are you able to keep your eyes on Christ and appreciate the ministry of various spiritual leaders without becoming an isolated follower of one man?

3. Apollos left Ephesus and was already ministering in Corinth when Paul arrived at Ephesus (Acts 19:1). On the second missionary journey, Paul wanted to minister to the people in the Roman province of Asia, but the Holy Spirit forbade him from going there (cf. Acts 16:6). No doubt Paul was excited when he realized that God finally did want him to minister to the people of Asia.

The Third Missionary Journey

   a. Paul met some disciples when he first arrived at Ephesus (Acts 19:1-3). Uncertain of their true identity, he asked them, "**Did you receive the Holy Spirit when you believed?**" (Acts 19:2). What do you think Paul was attempting to determine by this question (Jn. 3:5-8; Ro. 8:9)?

   b. What did their answer reveal about their spiritual identity (Acts 19:2-3)?

   c. How did these disciples respond when Paul explained Jesus to them (Acts 19:5-6)?

4. The apostle Paul entered the synagogue and continued to speak boldly for three months (Acts 19:8). When the Ephesian Jews rejected the truth, Paul withdrew himself and took his new disciples to the school of Tyrannus. (Note: Most Biblical scholars believe Tyrannus was a local philosopher of some notoriety.) For a period of two years, Paul taught these disciples daily (Acts 19:6).

   a. What were the results of Paul's teaching ministry to these disciples (Acts 19:10)?

   b. What NT churches were probably started during these two years (Col. 1:1-2; Rev. 2:1, 8, 12, 18; 3:1, 7, 14)?

5. By the time Paul arrived at Ephesus on his third missionary journey, the city had passed its zenith and was no longer the great commercial center of days past. Once located at the mouth of the Cayster River on the Aegean Sea, the harbor at Ephesus had been filled in due to silt deposits. Excessive lumbering and over grazing of the land had caused extensive erosion, and repeated attempts to clean the harbor had failed. (Note: The ancient harbor works of Ephesus now sit behind a swamp, seven miles from the Aegean Sea.) The city had begun to rely on other means of support.

   a. Many of the Ephesians had turned to magic arts, incantations, and exorcism in an attempt to make a living. Some of the Jews had become involved in these evil practices including the seven sons of a Jewish chief priest named Sceva (Acts 19:13-14). What happened when these seven men attempted to command the powers of darkness without the power of God in their lives (Acts 19:15-16)?

b. What happened when the people saw that there was a great difference between the power of God and the power of Satan (Acts 19:17-20)?

6. With the silting of the Ephesian harbor, the temple of Artemis had become the primary basis of Ephesus' wealth and continuing prosperity. Artemis was the grotesque multi-breasted goddess of fertility whom the Ephesians believed had fallen from heaven (cf. Acts 19:35). Located one and a half miles northwest of the city, the temple measured approximately four hundred by two hundred feet and was one of the Seven Wonders of the ancient world. The temple was four times larger than the Parthenon in Athens. It became a lucrative tourist attraction and an important banking center for those who sought the financial protection of the goddess. Local merchants were engaged in a profitable business selling miniature silver shrines to the tourists (Acts 19:24).

   a. During Paul's stay in Ephesus, he was joined by Timothy and a man named Erastus (Acts 19:21-22). Paul commissioned these two men to Macedonia for missionary service while he remained in Asia for a while (Acts 19:22). What happened during this time that nearly resulted in Paul's death (Acts 19:24-29)?

   b. The riot in Ephesus was the second recorded incident in the book of Acts provoked by Gentiles. What was the motive behind both these Gentile attacks (Acts 16:16-24; 19:24-25)?

7. The city of Ephesus was filled with confusion as two of Paul's traveling companions, Gauis and Aristarchus were dragged to the theater (Acts 19:29). (Note: The Ephesian theater was the largest place for an assembly in the city, capable of holding 25,000. Remains of this theater can be seen today). When Paul wanted to go into the assembly, he was restrained (Acts 19:30-31). Once again, God used civil government to solve a potentially deadly crowd and spare Paul and his friends. The term *city clerk* (Gr. *grammateus*, lit. scribe) was the chief executive officer of the city rather than a city registrar, as his name seems to imply (v 35). What three reasons did he give to quiet the crowd and cause them to dismiss in an orderly fashion (Acts 19:35-41)?

Study #4b The Third Missionary Journey

> Read - Acts 18:23-21:16; other references as given.

8. After Paul experienced great difficulties at Ephesus, he traveled north and passed through Macedonia into Greece (Acts 20:2) (Note: Greece was located south of Macedonia and north of Achaia.) When he spent three months there, he planned to sail back to Syria (i.e., Antioch and its environs), but a plot to kill him was discovered so he traveled by land back through Macedonia (Acts 20:3). (Note: Paul was carrying a financial gift from the churches to the churches of Judea who were experiencing poverty as a result of a famine [cf. 1 Cor. 16:1-3].) God used many lesser-known Christian workers to help evangelize the lost and to strengthen the churches. What significant observation can you make about this group of missionary helpers who accompanied Paul (Acts 20:4)?

9. Luke joined Paul at Philippi (cf. Acts 20:5) as they left Macedonia and landed at Troas in Asia Minor. (Note: This commences the second "we" section.) Luke states, **"Now on the first day of the week, when the disciples came together to break bread, Paul, ready to depart the next day, spoke to them ..."** (Acts 20:7). This is the clearest reference in the NT that indicates Sunday was the normal meeting day of the early church. Unfortunately, some Christians do not seem to understand the importance of gathering together each week in a local church where Christ is honored. Give at least three reasons why God's people should meet each week with other believers to worship God (Eph. 4:11-15; Heb. 10:23-25).

10. At Troas, Paul preached until midnight, and a young man named Eutychus fell asleep, fell out of a window, and died (Acts 20:7-9). After God used Paul to restore the man to life, he went back and preached until daybreak before he departed (Acts 20:10). At Miletus, Paul sent for the elders of the Ephesian church and addressed them as a group (Acts 20:17-35).

   a. God used Paul at Ephesus in a great way. In addition to his teaching responsibilities at the school of Tyrannus and in the various house churches (cf. Acts 20:20), Paul worked (probably tent making once again) to provide financial support for himself and others (cf. Acts 20:34-35). What else did Paul have to contend with during his time at Ephesus on the third missionary journey (Acts 20:19)?

The Third Missionary Journey

29

    b.   In Paul's sermon to the Ephesian elders, he mentions several things that made him a mighty servant of God. Name at least five (Acts 20:19-27, 33, 35).

11. Paul challenged the Ephesian elders or overseers to guard the church from spiritual harm. He said, **"For I know this, that after my departure savage wolves will come in among you, not sparing the flock."** (Acts 20:29).

    a.   To whom do you think he was referring by the phrase **"savage wolves"** (Acts 20:29; cf. 2 Cor. 11:12-15)?

    b.   Paul also warned the Ephesian elders to be on guard against another spiritual danger. What was it (Acts 20:30)?

    c.   What did Paul say to the Ephesian elders to assure them that they could effectively ward off the spiritual attacks (Acts 20:32)?

12. How did these Christian leaders respond to Paul's words (Acts 20:36-38)?

13. Paul sailed from Miletus to Patera where he found a pilgrim ship (i.e., one which carried both cargo and passengers) sailing to the city of Tyre in Syria (Acts 21:1-3). He stayed seven days with the disciples in Tyre who **"told Paul through the Spirit not to go up to Jerusalem"** (Acts 21:4). Apparently these believers knew that he would experience persecution or some other trouble if he went to Jerusalem.

a. Some Christians believe that the Holy Spirit still impresses future events upon the minds of believers. Do you believe that God reveals future events to His people in the same way He did to these disciples at Tyre? Why or why not?

b. The Holy Spirit has been given many ministries during this particular age: convicting the lost of sin and judgment (Jn. 16:8), interceding for the prayers of believers (Ro. 8:26). What else does the Holy Spirit do (Jn. 16:13)?

14. Paul left Ptolemais and arrived at Caesarea where he found Philip, one of the seven who had been chosen by the Jerusalem church to serve tables twenty years earlier (Acts 21:8). Philip had apparently settled in Caesarea, a predominately Gentile city. He now had four daughters who were prophetesses (Acts 21:9).

   a. A man named Agabus came down to Caesarea (about 65 miles) and tried to convince Paul not to go up to Jerusalem (Acts 21:12). Although Paul was still prepared to go to Jerusalem personally to deliver the financial gift from the churches of Macedonia, Achaia, and Asia Minor, who became convinced that he should not go (Acts 21:10-12)?

   b. What did Paul say in response to their appeal for him not to go to Jerusalem (Acts 21:13)?

   c. How did the people interpret Paul's determination to go to Jerusalem at all costs (Acts 21:14)?

Study #5a   Captured in Jerusalem

> Read - Acts 21:17-23:22; other references as given.

1. Paul arrived in Jerusalem at the end of the third missionary journey where the brethren received him gladly. On the following day, Paul met with James and the other leaders of the Jerusalem church and likely presented the financial gift that had been collected by the churches (cf. Acts 24:17) (Note: James, the half-brother of Christ was apparently still the spiritual leader of the Jerusalem congregation [cf. Acts 15:13; 1 Cor. 15:7; Ga. 2:9, 12].)

    a. Paul gave the spiritual leaders in Jerusalem an updated ministry report (Acts 21:19). When they heard his report, they began to glorify God (Acts 21:20). What did Paul emphasize in his testimony that made them respond this way (Acts 21:19)?

    b. When you give a testimony in a church service to another Christian or even to an unsaved person, are you careful to emphasize what God did rather than bringing glory to yourself?

2. The Judean brethren were glad to see Paul, and they must have been grateful to receive the financial gift as well (Acts 21:17). Nevertheless, they were concerned about his safety (Acts 21:20 ff.).

    a. The Jerusalem elders thought that a particular group of people might cause problems for Paul. Please identify this group? (Acts 21:20-21)?

    b. The Jerusalem leaders recommended a plan to Paul to avoid conflict with these potential protagonists. What was their plan (Acts 21:23-24)?

3. When the Jerusalem leaders told their plan to Paul, they restated their belief that the Gentiles were not obligated to keep the Law of Moses (Acts 21:25). (Note: The phrase, **"we have written"** refers to the elders' original letter to the church at

Antioch [cf. Acts 15:23-29].) Did the Jerusalem elders' plan go too far (i.e., a theological compromise leading to sin) in an attempt to avoid trouble with the Jews (Acts 21:23-26)? Why or why not?

4. Paul went along with the Jerusalem leaders' plan, but Jews from Asia (i.e., the ancient Roman province located on the western side of modern Turkey) began to stir up the multitude, and they took hold of him (Acts 21:27). The people dragged Paul out of the temple, immediately closed the doors behind him, and would have killed him if some Roman soldiers had not rescued him (Acts 21:30-33). Some Christians believe that Paul's trouble at this time is proof that the Jerusalem elders' plan was wrong. Do you think that Paul's immediate persecution at the hands of the Jews is proof that the Jerusalem elders' plan was wrong? Why or why not?

5. It is often difficult for Christians to determine how far they should go to meet the religious expectations of others. If a Christian is inflexible and unyielding, he can offend others and hinder his chances for future ministry. If he is willing to yield to any appeal, he compromises the truth and confuses the unsaved.

   a. If you, as a Christian, were asked by some family members or close friends to participate in the infant baptism of their child in which the minister told the audience that the baby became a Christian at the time of the baptism, what would you do?

   b. What could you do in this situation to maintain loyalty to Christ and a loving relationship with your family or friends as well?

6. There are several similarities between this riot in Jerusalem and the previous riot that occurred in Ephesus a few years earlier. Name at least three (Acts 19:28-41; 21:27-36).

7. Paul was rescued from the angry mob by some Roman soldiers who mistook him for an Egyptian insurrectionist and self-proclaimed prophet who had led a revolutionary army known as the Assassins (Acts 21:33-35, 38). According to Josephus, an early church historian, this man came to the Mount of Olives in 54 AD, promising his adherents that the walls of Jerusalem would collapse at his command. The Roman army marched on them and killed many before the remaining 4000 escaped into the wilderness (cf. Acts 21:37-38). When the Roman soldiers led Paul to the steps of the Antonio Fortress, which was located on the northwest corner of the Temple in Jerusalem, he asked to speak to the crowd (Acts 21:34, 37-40). What did Paul say to convince the Romans to let him speak to the people, and what did he do to quiet the people so he could speak to them (Acts 21:39-40)?

8. Paul's message to the Jews from the steps of the Antonio Fortress is a classic example of how a Christian should give his personal testimony. (Note: A personal testimony is the essential spiritual facts and events that surrounded a person's salvation.) It is important for every Christian to be able to share his salvation testimony in a logical, understandable manner. A personal testimony should begin with a few details about the historical events leading to salvation. Next, it should provide the listeners with the actual conversion events. Lastly, it should give some information of the difference Christ has made in the person's life.

   a. In Paul's salvation testimony to the Jews in Jerusalem (Acts 22:3-21), what verses comprise the first portion of his testimony (i.e., the events leading to salvation)?

   b. What verses describe Paul's actual conversion to Jesus Christ?

   c. What verses comprise the third portion of his testimony?

dy #5b — Captured in Jerusalem

> Read - Acts 21:17-23:22; other references as given.

9. Prior to Paul's salvation, he hunted down believers and imprisoned them (Acts 22:19). He even held the cloaks of those who stoned Stephen to death (Acts 22:20). Now, twenty years later, the hunter became the hunted as Paul attempted to defend his actions and testify of his conversion to Christ.

    a. What statement did Paul make that caused the Jewish mob to raise their voices and say, **"Away with such a fellow from the earth, for he is not fit to live!"** (Acts 22:22)?

    b. What happened to Paul next (Acts 22:24-26)?

10. Some twenty years after the stoning of Stephen, Paul still had a vivid recollection of the events of that gruesome event. Yet, he wrote to the Philippians, saying that he was **"forgetting those things which are behind"** (cf. Ph. 3:13).

    a. It does not seem like Paul was very successful at **"forgetting those things which are behind"** if he could still remember the events of Stephen's stoning about twenty years earlier. What do you think he meant by his statement to the Philippians (Ph. 3:12-14)?

    b. Sometimes Christians say that they know that God can forgive them for a particular sin, but they cannot forgive themselves. What do you think a believer can do to resolve this mental dilemma that can rob him of peace and render him ineffective for Christ?

    c. Is there a particular sin in your past that Satan has continued to use against you? What promise has God given you to assure you of His complete forgiveness (1 Jn. 1:9)?

d. Some Christians have struggled with tremendous feelings of guilt over past sins. They have confessed their sin to God many times, but they do not *feel* forgiven. What do you think a believer should do if he has confessed his sin to God, but he still does not feel forgiven for his sin?

11. Paul was released after nearly being flogged (Acts 22:30). But on the next day, the Roman commander (Gr. *chiliarch* - a commander of one thousand troops) brought the chief priests and the Council (i.e., the Sandehrin) together to examine Paul (Acts 22:30). When Paul addressed the Sandehrin as brothers, the high priest ordered him to be struck. (Note: Ananias, son of Nedebaeus, reigned as high priest from 48-58 or 59 AD and was known for avarice and violence.) How did Paul respond to this attack (Acts 23:3-5)?

12. Paul's comment to the high priest, **"God will strike you, you whitewashed wall!"** (Acts 23:3) turned out to be prophetic. Ananias was hunted as an animal and killed by his own people despite his scheming and bribes. If Paul readily apologized when he was told that he had spoken harshly to the high priest, why do you think he might not have been able to identify him before this incident (Ga. 4:12-15)?

13. Paul began his defense before the Sanhedrin by saying that he had lived his life **"in all good conscience before God until this day"** (Acts 23:1). It was important to Paul to have a good conscience before God and man (cf. Acts 24:16). Man's conscience is a gift from God that acts as a judge, reminding him of the Law of God (cf. Ro. 2:15). Conscience does not set the standard but only applies it to man's soul.

   a. Unfortunately, man can abuse his conscience to the point that it becomes largely ineffective in his life. The Bible describes several different types/conditions of man's conscience. Name at least four (1 Cor. 8:7; 1 Tim. 1:5; 3:9; 4:2; Ti. 1:15).

b. What are religious good works apart from salvation unable to do for man's conscience (Heb. 9:9)?

14. Man tries all sorts of things to avoid the voice of his conscience. He ignores it, he argues with it, he tries to silence it with drugs and alcohol, but it still speaks to him. As one philosopher said, "A guilty conscience is an early hell."

    a. What is the only thing that can cleanse a guilty conscience (Heb. 9:14)?

    b. Are you absolutely sure that your conscience has been washed clean by the blood of Jesus Christ? If you are not sure, ask your Pastor or Group Leader to help you.

15. The Sandehrin's interrogation of Paul took a new twist when he told them that he was a Pharisee and was on trial for the hope of the resurrection (Acts 23:6-10). The Pharisees, who believed in the resurrection, began to argue with the Sadducees who did not believe in the resurrection or angels. What religious group(s) do you think the Sadducees might be compared with today?

16. The debate between the Pharisees and the Sadducees escalated to the point that the Roman commander had to rescue Paul and take him back to the barracks (Acts 23:10).

    a. What was the Jews' plan to kill Paul at this time (Acts 23:12-15)?

    b. How did God protect Paul and fulfill his promise that said, **"so you must also bear witness at Rome"** (Acts 23:11, 16-22)?

Study #6a   Imprisoned at Caesarea

> Read - Acts 23:23-26:32; other references as given.

1. The apostle Paul was captured in the temple at Jerusalem by the Jews (cf. Acts 21:30). He was rescued from death by Roman soldiers who learned that he was a Roman citizen (cf. Acts 21:39). As a Roman citizen, the state was required to provide him certain rights and privileges, one of which was the right to due legal process. What did the Roman commander Claudius Lysias do when he found out that the Jews were plotting to kill Paul (Acts 23:23-30)?

2. Paul and the small army of men and horses traveled thirty-five miles northwest to Antipatris. (Note: Antipatris had been built by Herod the Great and named after his father.) Having left Jerusalem at the third hour of the night (9 p.m.), they reached their destination by the next day. At Antipathris, the infantry returned to Jerusalem while the cavalry escorted Paul to Caesarea, a distance of forty miles (Acts 23:33). Paul was delivered to Felix, the governor of Judea, along with the letter that Claudius Lysias sent. What did Felix say when he learned that Paul was from the neighboring Roman province of Cilicia (Acts 23:34-35)?

3. Only five days later, the high priest Ananias arrived from Jerusalem, bringing along with him some elders and an attorney named Tertullus (Acts 24:1).

    a. When Tertullus addressed Felix, he presented four accusations against Paul. What were they (Acts 24:2-6)?

    b. Tertullus also accused Claudius Lysias of wrongdoing. What did he say the Roman commander had done wrong (Acts 24:6, 7)?

4. Tertullus misrepresented the facts in order to make the Jews' case against Paul look better than it was. He falsely accused Paul of wrongdoing and Claudius Lysias of

obstructing justice. Since Felix was not present in Jerusalem during these events, it would have been difficult for him to know if Tertullus' accusations against Paul were accurate.

    a.   What did Felix do in order to determine the truth (Acts 24:10)?

    b.   What should a believer do when he hears only one side of a problem between two people (Pro. 18:17)?

    c.   What does the Bible say about the person who gives a quick answer before he has all the facts (Pro. 18:13)?

5.   a.   In Paul's defense before Felix (Acts 24:10-21), what do you observe about the difference between Paul's opening remarks and those of Tertullus (Acts 24:2-4, 10)?

    b.   What does the Bible teach about flattery (Pro. 7:21; 26:28; Ro. 16:18; Jude 16)?

6.   Paul told Felix that the accusations that the Jews had made could not be proved but the things that he was saying could be confirmed (Acts 24:11-14). Paul said, **"I myself always strive to have a conscience without offense toward God and men"** (Acts 24:16).

    a.   Name two things that every individual needs to do to have a blameless conscience before God (Heb. 9:11-14; 1 Jn. 1:9).

Imprisoned at Caesarea

b. What are three things that a believer needs to do to have a clear conscience before other men (Matt. 5:23-24; Ro. 12:17-18)?

7. What did Felix do after he had heard both sides of the controversy between the Jews and Paul (Acts 24:22-23)?

8. Several days after Paul's first defense before Felix in Caesarea, Paul was invited to speak to Felix and his wife Drusilla (Acts 24:24) (Note: Drusilla, Felix's third wife, was a Jewess who divorced her first husband Azizus, king of Emesa, to marry Felix while she was still a teen.)

   a. What was Felix's response when Paul spoke to him about the ethical implications of believing in God (Acts 24:24-25)?

   b. Felix was troubled by what Paul said to him, yet he invited him back several times to speak to him. Why did he continue to listen to Paul?

   c. Like Felix there are people today who will listen to the preaching of God's Word even though they are not saved. Why do you think some people attend church and listen to sermons if they are not saved and thus cannot understand the things of God (cf. 1 Cor. 2:14)?

Study #6b   Imprisoned at Caesarea

> Read - Acts 23:23-26:32; other references as given.

9. Felix was succeeded as governor of Judea by Porcius Festus two years after Paul was first imprisoned at Caesarea (Acts 24:27). All this time Paul had been held as prisoner, apparently without a formal trial (cf. Acts 25:26-27). Three days after Festus' arrival in Caesarea as the new governor, he went up to Jerusalem where the Jews brought **"many serious complaints against Paul, which they could not prove"** (Acts 25:7).

    a. At the time of Paul's original arrest in Jerusalem (cf. Acts 21:30 ff.), God assured him in a night vision that he would be His witness in Rome (cf. Acts 23:11). How did God use the wickedness of Festus to accomplish this objective (Acts 25:9-12)?

    b. Often God's people become discouraged when they see the wicked plans and schemes of godless men. They can be tempted to think that evil will prevail and God's plans will be thwarted. What does the Bible say about God's reaction to the wicked and their unrighteous plans (Ps. 2:1-5)?

10. Several days after Festus told Paul that he would be tried in Rome (i.e., Caesar), King Agrippa and his sister Bernice paid a diplomatic visit to Festus at Caesarea (Acts 25:13). (Note: Marcius Agrippa II was the great grandson of Herod the Great who sought to kill Jesus [cf. Matt. 2:1 ff.].) Bernice had been married to her uncle, but he had died and now she was living with her brother with whom she was accused both in Rome and Palestine of having an incestuous affair.

    a. When Festus sought Agrippa's advice concerning Paul's case, what did he say about the Jews' charges against Paul and about what Paul believed (Acts 25:18-19)?

    b. What do you think Festus' comments indicate about his own spiritual condition?

Imprisoned at Caesarea 41

11. When King Agrippa agreed to hear Paul, Agrippa was brought into the auditorium amid great pomp (Acts 25:23). Festus asked Agrippa, the commanders, and prominent men of the city to find some justifiable charge against Paul to send to Rome (Acts 25:24-27). Paul was given the opportunity to give his personal testimony to King Agrippa and others (Acts 26:2-23). Again, he presented the essential facts leading to his salvation in part one of his testimony, the actual events of his salvation experience in part two, and the critical events of his life since his conversion in part three. What verse references constitute part one, part two, and part three?

12. Every Christian should learn to give his personal testimony in a clear, organized manner. One effective way of giving your testimony is to identify the specific life need (e.g., fear of death, fear of going to hell, a feeling of purposelessness, etc.) in part one of the testimony. Part two should provide the essential details of the conversion experience, and part three should explain how Christ solved the life need identified in part one.

   a. What was your compelling life need before salvation that God used to bring you to Christ?

   b. The apostle Paul was saved at midday on a road north of Jerusalem (Acts 26:13 ff.). Where and when were you saved? If you are not sure of your salvation, see your Group Leader or Pastor and ask him or her to show you how you can receive the gift of eternal life.

   c. In what way(s) has Jesus Christ solved your concern about the life-need you identified in part one of your testimony?

13. In the third part of Paul's testimony (Acts 26:19 ff.), Paul states, "**I was not disobedient to the heavenly vision**" (Acts 26:19).

   a. What did he mean by this statement (Acts 26:16-20)?

b. If you are saved, God has called you to live a holy life and to make disciples of all nations (Acts 28:19-20; 1 Pe. 1:16). Can you say with the apostle Paul that you have been obedient to the things God has shown you?

c. If not, what do you think you need to do to fulfill God's will for your life?

14. Some Christians think that if they witness for Christ and testify of His saving work on the cross, their listeners will respond with repentance. While this happens more than most non-witnessing Christians realize (cf. Matt. 9:37; Jn. 4:35), some people will resist the grace of God and reject His offer of eternal life.

   a. Both Festus and Agrippa rejected the message of salvation through faith in Christ. While their responses to the gospel were unfortunate, they are typical of the kinds of answers witnessing Christians can often expect today. What were their specific responses (Acts 26:24, 28)?

   b. How did Paul respond to Festus' accusation that he was crazy (Acts 26:25-27)?

15. The apostle Paul refused to be silenced. He loved the Lord Jesus Christ too much to be disobedient to His commands, and he loved the lost too much not to warn them of the coming judgment of God. Do you love Jesus Christ enough to be faithful to witness to the lost even if it means facing rejection and ridicule?

Study #7a   The Journey to Rome

>Read - Acts 27:1-28:31; other references as given.

1. Paul was imprisoned at Caesarea for over two years, but he experienced some degree of liberty (cf. Acts 24:23, 27). After this, Paul was placed on a pilgrim ship (i.e., one carrying both cargo and passengers) that was scheduled to make stops along the western coast of Asia Minor (Acts 27:1-2). (Note: Adramyttium was a seaport of Mysia on the northwest coast of Asia Minor.) Name two of Paul's missionary co-workers who accompanied him on this perilous journey (Acts 27:1-2).

2. Christians can become discouraged when they encounter trials; however, it is during these times that God often provides His "tender mercies," those special blessings, to encourage the hearts of His people. In addition, trials often help God's people become more alert to what He is doing in their lives.

    a. God providentially arranged for two of Paul's missionary companions to accompany him on his journey to Rome. How else did God provide for Paul during this time (Acts 27:1-3; cf. Col. 4:14)?

    b. Now think of a trial that you have experienced (health, financial, work related, etc.). How did God assure you of His love and care during this time? (Note: Be prepared to testify in your group of God's love and goodness toward you.)

3. Although it is not stated, Paul and the rest of the passengers likely sailed from Caesarea. They would have traveled seventy miles north along the Mediterranean coast to Sidon (Acts 27:3). From Sidon, they traveled northwest toward Cyprus and sailed along the north side of the island to be protected from the prevailing easterly winds that blow over the Mediterranean Sea from spring to fall. They continued westward toward the city of Myra in Lycia (a Roman province), helped along by the westerly current that flows along the southern shore of Asia Minor. At Mysia, they were transported to another ship headed for Italy, their final destination. From Mysia, they traveled slowly many days and arrived with difficulty (Acts 27:7-8). Do you think the difficulty they experienced during their trip was an indication that God did not want Paul to go to Rome? Why or why not (cf. Acts 23:11)?

4. When some Christians encounter trials or adversity, they almost automatically think that their troubles are a result of some past sin or failure. If this happens, the individual often experiences unnecessary guilt.

   a. Give five Biblical reasons God's people experience adversity in their lives (Jn. 16:33; Gal. 6:7-8; Eph. 6:11-12; Heb. 12:5-10; 1 Pet. 4:12-13).

   b. How can a believer tell if the trouble he is experiencing is the result of some sin he needs to repent of, an individual trial of faith in which he needs to endure joyfully, or just the everyday consequences of living in a fallen world (Ps. 139:23; Jn. 8:32)?

5. The ship upon which Paul and the other 275 people were traveling docked at a place called Fair Havens (modern Limeonas Kalous) on the southern shore of the island of Crete (Acts 27:8, 37). Navigation in this part of the Mediterranean Sea was considered dangerous after September 14th and considered impossible after November 11th. The Jewish fast (i.e., the day of atonement), held on the 10th day of the lunar month Tishri (i.e., the last part of September and the first part of October in a solar calendar), was already past (Acts 27:9).

   a. Give two reasons why the captain and the Roman centurion decided to sail from Fair Havens to Phoenix (a distance of forty miles) even though Paul warned them against it (Acts 27:10-13)?

   b. What happened as a result of their fateful decision (Acts 27:14-20)?

   c. What did Paul say to encourage the other passengers when they thought all was lost (Acts 27:21-26)?

6. Paul's words, **"Men, you should have listened to me"** (Acts 27:21) appear to violate a basic rule of effective communication: don't remind others in a time of trouble of their failure to follow your advice. Why do you think Paul reminded the people, especially those in charge of the ship, of their failure (cf. Acts 27:10, 21-32)?

7. Paul was reminded by God that he would stand before Caesar (Acts 27:24). In God's statement to Paul, He says, **"God has granted you all those who sail with you."** What do you think this indicates about Paul's concern for the welfare of those on the ship?

8. The sailors planned to escape the impending shipwreck by getting into the ship's boat (i.e., a dingy) and pretending to lay out anchors from the ship's bow (Acts 27:30). When Paul warned the sailors that their plan would end in death, they abandoned their plan and cut the dingy loose (Acts 27:31-32). Paul encouraged the people to take some food since it was fourteen days since they had eaten (Acts 27:33-36). Give several evidences of God's providential care for Paul and all the people during the shipwreck (Acts 27:39-44).

Study #7b   The Journey to Rome

> Read - Acts 27:1-28:31; other references as given.

9. The lives of all 276 people were saved from the shipwreck on the island of Malta, which is located 58 miles south of Sicily. (Note: The island is 18 miles long and 8 miles wide.) The islands had been colonized about 1000 BC by Phoenicians and conquered by Rome in 218 BC. It had been given the status of a *municipium*, which afforded the islanders a measure of local self-government under the leadership of a local governor or "chief man". At the time of the shipwreck, Publius occupied this leadership role on the island (cf. Acts 28:7).

   a. The writer Luke refers to the Maltese islanders as natives (Gr. *barbario* - barbarians). The Greek word (*barbario*) is an onomatopoetic word; to the Greeks and Romans strange languages sounded like "bar-bar-bar," hence the work barbarian. What happened on Malta that made the islanders think Paul to be a murderer (Acts 28:3-4)?

   b. What did the islanders think when Paul did not die from the viper's bite (Acts 28:5-6)?

10. This incident on Malta is an excellent example of the fallacy of attempting to determine truth from personal experience alone. Unfortunately, some modern Christians duplicate the error of these ancient people.

    a. If a Christian attempts to assign arbitrary meaning to various situations in life apart from God's Word, in what is he trusting?

    b. The Maltese islanders' method of determining truth (i.e., a subjective human interpretation) is commonly known as mysticism. Give at least three practical reasons mysticism is an incorrect way to determine truth.

11. Publius, the chief official of the island, provided food and lodging for the victims of the shipwreck (Acts 28:7). God used Paul to heal Publius' father from recurring fever and dysentery (Acts 28:8) and others with various diseases (Acts 28:9). Three months later at the beginning of the next shipping season, Paul and the others boarded a ship from Alexandria, North Africa that had been moored at Malta over the winter (Acts 28:11).

   a. After a brief stay at Syracuse and Puteoli, they finally arrived at Rome (Acts 28:12-14). When Paul, Luke, and Aristarchus arrived in Rome, brethren from the **Appii Forum** (43 miles away) and **Three Inns** (33 miles away) encouraged Paul by visiting (Acts 28:15). What happened three days after Paul arrived in Rome (Acts 28:16-22)?

   b. Without any formal charges or even accusations against him, Paul was probably very close to being released. What did he do when the leading Jews of the area requested to hear his views (Acts 28:22-23)?

   c. What was the spiritual response to his message to the Jews?

12. How did Paul respond to those who rejected the gospel message (Acts 28:25-28)?

13. Although the Jews again rejected the message of eternal life, Paul stayed two full years in his own rented quarters, **"preaching the kingdom of God and teaching the things which concern the Lord Jesus Christ with all confidence"** (Acts 28:31). The final aspect of Jesus' command to the apostles to be His witnesses, **"in Jerusalem, and in all Judea and Samaria, and to the end of the earth"** (Acts 1:8) was complete.

   a. What spiritual qualities of the early church apostles and missionaries do you admire most? Why?

b. The effective expansion of the early church was greatly aided by the valuable contribution of many lesser known saints who served their Lord Jesus and others so valiantly (e.g., Barnabas, Silas, John Mark, Aquilla, Priscilla, Apollos, Titus, Aristarchus, Luke, Stephen, Philip, etc.). Which one(s) of these lesser-known saints was a special spiritual encouragement to your Christian life?

Congratulations.

You have just finished the second half of the Lamplighters study of Acts. By completing all eighteen lessons in this study, you should have a better understanding of the expansion of the early church. You should also have a better understanding of the sacrifices the early believers made to proclaim the message of salvation. Now two thousand years later, Jesus Christ still commands His people, **"You shall be witnesses to me both in Jerusalem, and in all Judea and Samaria, and to the end of the earth"** (Acts 1:8). Like the apostles, the church today needs to answer the question that the angels asked the apostles, **"Men of Galilee, why do you stand gazing up into heaven?" (Acts 1:11).** May God help us to love Jesus Christ and those he died to save and to reach out with the message of His redeeming love.

Study #1a   The First Missionary Journey

1. 1. Barnabas was a generous man who was willing to use his material possessions for the advancement of the gospel (Acts 4:35).
   2. Barnabas had the ability to encourage others in the Lord (Acts 4:36).
   3. Barnabas was a good man, full of the Holy Spirit and faith (Acts 11:22, 24).
   4. Barnabas, a wise leader, realized the need to involve others in the teaching ministry of the believers at Antioch (Acts 11:25).
   5. Barnabas and Paul demonstrated effective spiritual leadership in the church at Antioch prior to their call (Acts 11:26).
   6. Barnabas and Paul were also busy serving in the church from which the Holy Spirit called them (Acts 13:2).

2. The spiritual magnitude of world missions necessitates the prayer support of God's people. Some independent missionaries fail to gather the prayer support of God's people that is essential to spiritual effectiveness in missionary work. All missionaries should be accountable to the local church, which is another important aspect of missionary work. Other answers could apply.

3. The believer should pray for God's mercy. Although there are examples in the Bible of God's people asking Him to bring judgment upon their spiritual enemies, the Christian should not use these examples as a pattern to follow. Sometimes the OT psalmists asked God to exact judgment on their enemies. (Note: These psalms are commonly known as the imprecatory psalms.) Under the OT Mosaic covenant, God obligated Himself to defend His people against their enemies if His people would obey the stipulations of the covenant (cf. Dt. 28); however, in the New Testament, Jesus Christ taught in the Sermon on the Mount (Matt. 5-7) that God's people are to bless those who curse and persecute them (Matt. 5:10-11). The apostles (Acts 4:8 ff.), Stephen (Acts 8:60), and Paul (1 Cor. 4:12-13) followed Christ's teaching and manifested an attitude of spiritual non-retaliation. However, a notable exception was when the apostle Paul said he delivered to Satan for the destruction of his flesh a man living in an immoral situation and unwilling to repent (cf. 1 Cor. 5:4-5). Regarding the incident with Bar-Jesus, it is likely that Paul was acting as God's apostolic representative when he pronounced judgment upon Bar-Jesus. This is hardly a position that an ordinary believer should assume.

4. a. 1. The Jewish leaders did not recognize Jesus as the Messiah (Acts 13:26).
      2. The Jewish leaders did not understand the words of the prophets (Acts 13:26).

- 5.
  - b.
    - 3. The Jewish leaders killed Jesus just as the prophets had predicted (Acts 13:29).
  - b. Paul warned the people of Pisidian Antioch to be careful so that God's judgment did not come upon them.
- 5. a.
  - 1. Many of the Jews begged Barnabas and Paul to tell them the same things the next Sabbath (v. 42).
  - 2. The people followed them (v. 43).
  - 3. All the people of the city gathered together to hear them (v. 44).
  - 4. Some of the Jews (probably the Jewish leaders) were filled with jealousy and were blaspheming (Acts 13:45).
  - 5. These Jewish leaders stirred up the prominent women and the leading men of the city and instigated a persecution, which drove Barnabas and Paul out of the city (Acts 13:50).
  - b. Answers will vary.
- 6. Paul and Barnabas interpreted the Jews' rejection of the gospel as God's will to turn their spiritual attention to the Gentiles. They believed Isaiah's prophecy (cf. Acts 13:47; Is. 42:6) applied to them directly ("the Lord has commanded *us*").
- 7. a. A believer should speak boldly or confidently with reliance upon the Lord. This means that he should not trust in his own ability to speak or persuade men but he should rely upon the Holy Spirit to guide him as he speaks. He should also trust Jesus Christ to work in the hearts of those who heard the message of salvation, trusting God to convict and convince of sin and the need for salvation.
  - b.
    - 1. There shouldn't be any use of human wisdom that contradicts the wisdom of God (1 Cor. 2:1).
    - 2. There should not be any use of deceit or mental manipulation (Acts 13:10).
    - 3. There should not be any gainsaying, which is religious teaching motivated by a desire to exploit others for the personal financial advantage of the teacher (Titus 1:10-11).
  - c. Answers will vary.
- 8. a.
  - 1. The Jews who did not accept the message of salvation stirred up the minds of the Gentiles and embittered them against those who had been saved (Acts 14:2).
  - 2. Some people believed the missionaries, and others did not (Acts 14:4).
  - 3. Some of the Jews and Gentiles who did not believe the gospel tried to mistreat Barnabas and Paul, even attempting to stone them (Acts 14:5).
  - b. They fled to the cities of Lycaonia, Lystra, Derbe, and the surrounding region where they continued to preach the gospel.
- 9. a. "Follow Me, and I will make you become fishers of men."
  - b.
    - 1. A Christian must first learn to follow Christ first of all.

Study #1b   The First Missionary Journey

10. a. **"We also are men of the same nature as you, and preach to you, that you should turn from these useless things to the living God, who made the heaven, the earth, the sea, and all things that are in them."**
    b. 1. Pastors and Bible teachers should be quick to give glory to God for every spiritual benefit others gain as a result of their ministries.
       2. They should also admit their faults and errors to others. (Note: A Christian leader needs to exercise wisdom as to when and to whom he admits his shortcomings so that others do not lose complete confidence in him as a leader.)
       3. They should teach expository so that God and His Word are exalted rather than the perceived intellect of the teacher.
       4. They should seek to honor others rather than themselves. Other answers could apply.
    c. God had given them rains from heaven and fruitful seasons. He also satisfied them with food and given them gladness.

11. They gathered the church together and reported all that God had done through them. They told the church how God had opened the door for effective ministry. They stayed an unspecified time with the church at Antioch.

12. a. Some men came from Judea and began teaching the believers at Antioch that they needed to be circumcised according to the Law of Moses in order to be saved. Paul and Barnabas disagreed with them, and a great disagreement arose between these teachers and Paul and Barnabas.

    b. Paul and Barnabas taught that people did not need to adhere to the OT Mosaic Law in order to be saved. They had been teaching that forgiveness of sins came through Jesus Christ (v. 38). They also said that the one who trusts Christ is freed from all things, from which they could not be freed through the Law of Moses (v. 39).

13. a. 1. No man is righteous before God (Ro. 3:10).
       2. No man truly understands God (Ro. 3:11).
       3. No man truly seeks for God (Ro. 3:11).
       4. No man is useful to God in his natural state (Ro. 3:12).
       5. No man does well in the eyes of God (Ro. 3:12).

    6. No man's speech is acceptable and pure in the eyes of God (Ro. 3:13).
    7. All men are guilty before God and cannot offer a legitimate excuse for their sin because the Law of God has condemned every man (Ro. 3:19).
    8. Every man has sinned and has fallen short of the standard that God established for entrance into heaven (Ro. 3:23).
  b. Answers will vary.

14. As they traveled through Phoenicia and Samaria, they met believers along the way whom they encouraged by telling them of the conversion of the Gentiles. Paul and Barnabas' ministry to these Christians must have been particularly encouraging because it caused great (Gr. *mega*) joy not just to a few, but to *all* the brethren (Acts 15:3). (Note: If a Christian can remain sensitive to the leading of the Holy Spirit and trust God to use him as he goes through life, he will find that God will use him to be a great spiritual encouragement to others. Rather than trying to manufacture ministry, he will be *"useful for the Master, prepared for every good work"* [cf. 2 Tim. 2:21].)

15. They were Jewish believers who had maintained a certain degree of allegiance and affiliation to the sect of the Pharisees even though they were now part of the church. These believers were confused about the relationship of law and grace even though they were saved themselves.

16. a. Paul and Barnabas.
  b. 1. Peter said God had originally chosen him to preach to the Gentiles so that they might believe (v. 7).
    2. Peter said that God, who knows the hearts of all men, confirmed his ministry to the Gentiles by giving them the Holy Spirit, just as He did for the Jews (v. 8).
    3. Peter said God made no distinction between the Jews and the Gentiles, cleansing both groups by faith (v. 9).
  c. **"Now therefore, why do you test God by putting a yoke on the neck of the disciples which neither our fathers nor we were able to bear?"**

17. James quoted from the prophets Isaiah, Jeremiah, and Amos to prove that what was taking place (i.e., the salvation of the Gentiles) was consistent with what God's Word had said.

18. 1. James recommended to the church in Jerusalem that they should not force the Gentile believers to observe the regulations of the OT Mosaic Law (v. 19).
  2. James also recommended that a letter be sent to the believers in Antioch that would explain their position and ask them to abstain from things contaminated by idols, from fornication, from what is strangled, and from blood (v. 20).

19. The apostles and elders' letter was a great encouragement to the believers at Antioch, bringing them great joy (v. 31).

Study #2a   The Second Missionary Journey

1. A disagreement arose between Paul and Barnabas about whether John Mark should accompany them on the second missionary journey. Even though John Mark had deserted them on the first missionary journey, Barnabas wanted to give him a second chance. Paul kept insisting that he not be allowed to accompany them (v. 38). When Barnabas and Paul could not resolve their problem, they decided to separate and go their own ways (v. 39).

2. a. 1. At the end of Paul's life, he asked Timothy to bring John Mark with him when Timothy came to visit Paul. Paul said that John Mark was profitable for ministry - an obvious endorsement of John's Christian character and substantial evidence that he had been effectively restored to spiritual usefulness (2 Tim. 4:11).
    2. God allowed John Mark to be the one whom the Holy Spirit used to write the gospel bearing his name.
  b. Answers will vary.

3. 1. Timothy was a believer (Acts 16:1).
  2. Timothy had a good Christian reputation in both Lystra and Iconium. The fact that Timothy had a good spiritual reputation in both cities is significant because it shows that his virtuous Christian testimony witness had extended beyond his friends and family. As one commentator said, "We all have a few prejudiced friends who have an undying faith in us."
  3. Timothy had been well taught in the Holy Scriptures as a child (2 Tim. 3:15).

4. 1. A church should carefully evaluate the Christian character of all missionary candidates to make certain that they meet the Biblical qualifications for spiritual leadership (cf. 1 Tim. 3:1-7; Titus 1:5-9).
  2. A church should check personal references to gain a broader perspective of the missionary candidate's character.
  3. The church should seek to endorse only those individuals who have already demonstrated spiritual effectiveness in their present local church ministries. It makes very little sense to endorse an individual who plans to serve the Lord in a foreign country when he is not actively serving the Lord in his own local church.

4. The church should endorse only those missionary candidates who have already demonstrated effectiveness in the area of personal evangelism and discipleship. A missionary candidate who is shy or fearful about sharing the gospel will not be an effective servant of God on a foreign field until he is willing to trust God to overcome his weakness. Other answers could apply.

5. a. Paul wanted Timothy to be circumcised because it would have been a stumbling block to the Jews who were living in the area of Lystra, Derbe, and Iconium (v. 3). Many of the unsaved Jews in that area knew that Timothy's father was a Greek and his mother was a Jew. If Timothy had not been circumcised, it would likely have been a poor testimony to the Jews and a hindrance to the spread of the gospel. From Paul's perspective, being a good Christian witness did not mean being a bad Jew. Paul had a great desire to see his countrymen saved, and he was willing to go as far as he could within the limits of Biblical authority to see them converted (1 Cor. 9:19-23). Timothy's circumcision had nothing to do with his salvation.
   b. The church of Jesus Christ should adapt itself to the culture in which God has placed it as long as it does not violate Scripture. Historically, the church has had the tendency to either separate itself from the world to the point of cultural isolation or it has become so immersed in the culture that it loses its witness for Christ. Some churches have become largely ineffective in their world outreach because they have made certain passing cultural issues into "fundamentals" of the faith. Others have allowed the changing social norms of a decaying society (e.g., acceptance of homosexuality, ordination of women pastors, etc.) to dictate their interpretation of Scripture. The former error leads to a cultural irrelevance and the latter error leads to compromise and worldliness.

6. a. The three missionaries were forbidden by the Holy Spirit (v. 6; cf. Spirit of Jesus, v. 7) to speak the Word of God in Asia. The Text does not say how the Holy Spirit communicated His will to the missionaries. Perhaps, it was through Silas, a prophet (cf. Acts 15:32).
   b. 1. Paul sought the godly counsel of others ("we" [v. 10]).
      2. He and others employed their mental capacities to interpret the vision's meaning (concluding, Gr. *sumbibadzo* - to put together in one's mind, to consider, to conclude [v. 1]). Paul did not mystically assign an arbitrary meaning to the vision independent of the godly counsel of others or apart from the careful reflection of God's Word.
   c. On many occasions a believer should seek the wise counsel of dedicated Christians to help him determine the will of God for his life. He should also employ his own mental capabilities so that he gets a Biblical perspective on a specific question. (Additional Note: It has been said that 90% of God's will for the believer is clearly stated in 100% of God's Word. If a believer faces a question regarding God's will for his life that does not appear to be directly

addressed in Scripture, he should seek to determine the various Biblical principles that pertain to the question then prayerfully seek God, trusting Him to lead him in a plain path (cf. Pro. 3:5-6; Ro. 12:1-2).

7. a. 1. The missionaries stayed in the city for some days (v. 12). This allowed them time to recuperate from their journey and the opportunity to plan the most effective way to evangelize the city.
   2. During this time they likely learned that there was no synagogue in the city since they planned to go to the designated place of Jewish prayer (v. 13). (Note: The Jewish population at Philippi must have been quite small since the presence of ten heads of household in a city required them to build a synagogue. It appears that the Jews and Gentile proselytes met at a specified Jewish place of prayer which was near the Gangites River, Philippi's only river.)
   b. 1. God providentially brought a lady named Lydia from Thyatira to Philippi at the same time Paul and his companions came there to spread the gospel.
   2. The missionaries spoke to Lydia and other women about their need for salvation.
   3. The Lord saved her and her household (v. 14).
   4. She invited the missionaries to stay with her, thus providing accommodations for the itinerant missionaries (v. 15).
   5. The Lord allowed a church to be started and to be organized according to the NT pattern (Ph. 1:1).
   6. The Philippian church generously supported Paul while he ministered in other cities (Ph. 4:15-16).

8. a. 1. It is likely that the constant crying out of the slave-girl was a distraction to the ministry.
   2. Undoubtedly, Paul and his companions did not want to be identified with the demonized woman and her masters who were using her demonic powers for financial gain (v. 19).
   3. God is never glorified by the work of Satan, nor does He need the assistance of Satan to accomplish His work. Other answers could apply.
   b. When the slave-girl's masters saw that their hope of profit was gone, they seized Paul and Silas and brought them before the authorities (v. 19). These wicked men falsely accused Paul and Silas before the chief magistrates who had the missionaries beaten with rods (vv. 22-23). The two missionaries were thrown into prison with their feet fastened in stocks (v. 24).

Study #2b   The Second Missionary Journey

9. a. This expression refers to the joy and peace that believers can have during a trial. When a believer rejoices during a trial, God has given him the ability to see beyond his present difficulties to the One who controls the trial. Faith enables the believer to praise Him (**songs in the night**), not because he finds pleasure in the trial itself, but because God gives him the grace to trust Him who governs every trial.
   b. Answers will vary.

10. a. Believing in the Lord Jesus means that an individual is trusting Jesus Christ alone for eternal life. The individual places his faith in the finished work of Jesus Christ on the cross as a payment for his sin debt to God. When a person truly recognizes his sinful condition before God, admits that he cannot redeem himself through good deeds, and calls upon Jesus Christ once for all to save his lost soul, he is saved. This salvation is an eternal deliverance from the wrath of God that abides on all men who have never trusted Christ. The phrase "you and your household" is emphasizing the universality of Christ's offer of redemption. It is not teaching "household salvation" because every person must call upon the name of Jesus Christ individually (cf. Jn. 1:12; Ro. 10:13).
    b. The jailer and his household were baptized, having believed in God with all his household (v. 34). The single Greek word (*pepisteukos* - perfect act. participle), from which the phrase "having believed" is translated, indicates that individual faith in the message of salvation (**"believed in God"** [v. 34]) was exercised before they were baptized. This proves that those who were baptized were old enough to understand the message and be saved.

11. a. 1. Reasoned (Gr. *dielexato* - to teach with a method of questions and answers with the goal of intellectual stimulus). Paul entered into a spiritual dialogue with the people, using the Scriptures as his authority.
      2. Explaining (Gr. *dianoigon* - to open) - Paul offered spiritual explanations to the normal questions (voiced or not voiced) that unsaved people often have before they are willing to trust Christ. By doing so, he opened their minds to the person of Jesus Christ.
      3. Demonstrating (Gr. *paratithememos* - to place alongside, to bring forward Biblical proof of the doctrine). Paul's presentation was not just an emotional appeal but it was the systematic presentation of Biblical truth to the people.
      4. Preach (Gr. *kataggello* - to proclaim with force). Paul heralded the message of Christ's salvation in a manner that highlighted its importance and the urgency to accept God's free gift of eternal life before it was too late.
   b. 1. Some of the Jews, a great multitude of God-fearing Greeks, and a number of the leading women were saved (v. 4). These people continued to follow the spiritual leadership of Paul and Silas.

Leader's Guide 57

        2. Most of the Jews became jealous and secured wicked men from the marketplace to form a mob that set the city in an uproar (v. 5).
        3. The mob went looking for the missionaries at the house of a man named Jason.

12. a. 1. They said the missionaries had upset the whole world (v. 6).
        2. They said that there is another king, Jesus (v. 7).
   b. Answers will vary.
   c. 1. Pray. 2. Live a dedicated Christian life. 3. Actively seek to win the lost to Christ. 4. Sacrifice financially to support missionaries. Other answers could apply.

13. a. 1. The Bereans received the Word with great eagerness. 2. They examined the Scriptures daily. 3. They evaluated the preaching of the missionaries according to the written revelation that they possessed.
   b. Answers will vary but could include: a lack of commitment, sin, worldly values that choke out the spiritual priorities of life. Other answers could apply.
   c. Answers will vary but could include the following: 1. Make a commitment to study the Bible every day. 2. Pray for God's grace to help you be faithful in this important area of your Christian life. 3. Ask another Christian to pray for you. 4. Begin a systematic Bible study or Bible reading schedule that provides an outline of your daily study responsibilities. Other answers could apply.

Study #3a   The Second Missionary Journey

1. a. Paul saw a city full of idols (Acts 17:16). Paul knew that behind the idols were demons who were being worshipped by the idolaters whether they realized it or not (1 Cor. 10:19-20). (Note: It was said that there were so many idols in ancient Athens that it was easier to find a man than a certain idol in the city.)
   b. 1. Paul's spirit was provoked when he saw the idolatry of the Athenians (v. 16).
      2. He went to the synagogue and reasoned with the Jews and the God-fearing Gentiles (v. 17).
      3. He went to the marketplace and reasoned with those who happened to be present, including some of the Epicurean and Stoic philosophers (vv. 17-18).

2. 1. The church should become a more active force in the preservation and restoration of society by boldly preaching the gospel of Jesus Christ to the lost. When men are brought to salvation through faith in Jesus Christ, they

experience the life-transforming power of God that inevitably produces significant social change.
2. Christians should also become involved in the political process, electing men and women who will support legislation that promotes righteous living.
3. They should also work for social change through community involvement, but they must remember that man's greatest need is eternal redemption, not temporary reformation.

3. There are a variety of secular philosophies that emphasize happiness as man's chief goal in life. Secular humanism is a modern philosophy that denies the reality of eternity and encourages man to pursue those objectives that supposedly give happiness and personal peace. The modern "death with dignity" philosophy, which is often promoted among the terminally ill, gives many patients and family a false sense of assurance regarding the patient's existence after life. Society's departure from the absolute standards of truth have led many to adopt an existential, feeling based, priority in decision-making. This had led many people in modern society to view truth as relative rather than objective. Other answers could apply.

4.
1. The Stoics' theological perspective of pantheism is reflected in the modern New Age movement, which believes that god can be found in everything.
2. The Stoics' belief in a resilient self-determination in the face of difficulty is seen in the secularism of modern humanism that denies the need for God and seeks to overcome the trials of life through human fortitude and mental discipline.
3. The commendation of suicide as an honorable means of escaping the emptiness and anguish of life is seen in some rock music and the more current attempts to legitimize active euthanasia. Other answers could apply.

5.
a. Paul responded with silence. Likely, he realized that their foolish comments were a product of their lost spiritual condition. He chose to remain silent at this time so that he would not engage in a fruitless argument nor forfeit the opportunity to address them publicly at a later time. God used Paul's initial response (i.e., silence) to cause the secular philosophers to invite him to address them on Mars Hill.
b. Christians should not always respond to every negative comment about God or those who stand against God's truth. Sometimes God's people think that they must stand up for Christ in every situation when truth is maligned. While this attitude is commendable, they should realize that many of the critical statements that unsaved people make are simply fiery darts from Satan that need to be defended by the shield of faith (cf. Eph. 6:10, 16). The Bible tells Christians **"Blessed are you when they revile and persecute you ... Rejoice and be exceedingly glad, for great is your reward in heaven..."** (Matt. 5:11-12). However, there are times when the Christian's silent response to a disparaging spiritual comment might be misconstrued as

either passive agreement or spiritual cowardice. Knowing when and how to answer the foolish comments of others takes great wisdom and discernment as the book of Proverbs so appropriately teaches, **"Do not answer a fool according to his folly, Lest you also be like him. Answer a fool according to his folly, Lest he be wise in his own eyes."** (Pro. 26:4). May God give His people the wisdom to know how to apply this great spiritual truth.

6. a. Paul observed the objects of their worship. Since everyone worships either the true God of heaven or the false gods of this world, a Christian can often identify the object of an individual's worship if he is observant. If nothing is obvious, the believer can identify the object of a person's worship by engaging an individual in conversation. These observations can help an alert Christian serve more effectively for Christ.
   b. Answers will vary.

7. 1. Peter quoted from the Scriptures several times (Acts 2:17-20, 25-28, 34-35) but did not use one OT reference.
   2. Paul quoted from a secular source (Acts 17:28) but Peter used no secular sources.
   3. Peter's message began with an explanation of the Holy Spirit's work through the apostles (Acts 2:15-18), while Paul's message began with an observation of the religious devotion of the Athenians (Acts 17:22 ff.).
   4. Peter's message focused on the true identity of Jesus as Lord and Christ (Acts 2:36), but Paul's message focused on the true identity of God the Father (Acts 17:24-29).
   5. Peter's message emphasized the Jews' need for repentance due to their unwillingness to accept the Lord Jesus Christ as the Messiah (Acts 2:23, 36). Paul's message emphasized the Athenian's need for repentance based upon the coming judgment of God (Acts 17:30-31). Other answers could apply.

Study #3b   The Second Missionary Journey

8. Paul emphasized the same elements as Peter did at Pentecost. Both messages emphasize the true identification of God and man's need for repentance. In Paul's address to the Athenians, he does not use a philosophical approach that emphasizes rational argumentation. He places God and His nature at the forefront of his presentation (cf. Acts 17:24). He explains who God is, what He has done for man, what He expects of those He created, and why He patiently waits for man to repent (Acts 17:24-31). While it is truth that Paul's message is distinctive from Peter's sermon to the Jews at Pentecost, he still preached the gospel of Jesus Christ, and people were saved (cf. Acts 17:34).

9.
1. Human wisdom (i.e., the wisdom of this world) has never been able to bring man to the knowledge of God (1 Cor. 1:21), but God has been pleased to use the message of the gospel to save those who believe.
2. Some men attempt to find God through mystical signs (e.g., the Jews) and others attempt to understand God by means of human logic (e.g., Greeks), but the message of Christ's finished work on the cross is the power of God to everyone who believes (1 Cor. 1:24). What a glorious unchangeable message of hope!

10.
1. God has placed in every man's mind the reality of eternal existence (Ecc. 3:11).
2. The Lord Jesus Christ is drawing all men to Him (Jn. 12:32).
3. God has placed a conscience in the heart of every man that reminds him of the law of God, which He uses to convict men of right and wrong (Ro. 2:14-15).

11.
a. God was patient toward man and had not yet executed the divine judgment upon them in relationship to their sin. God withholds his judgment upon mankind because He understands that his spiritual ignorance is a result of the effects of sin and Satan's deception.
b.
1. God has appointed a specific day when Jesus Christ will righteously judge the world. Christ became qualified to serve in this capacity as judge of the world when He was raised from the dead (Acts 17:31).
2. All men will perish unless they repent (Lu. 13:3).
3. There is no other way to be saved (Acts 4:12).
c.
1. Some jeered (v. 32).
2. Others wanted to hear more at another time (v. 32).
3. Some followed Paul and came to faith some time after hearing Paul's message (v. 34).

12.
a. Paul was weak (1 Cor. 2:3). Perhaps this reference to Paul's weakness not only refers to his physical struggles he was facing as a result of his travels and the beating he received at Philippi (cf. Acts 16:22-23), but also the emotional fatigue he was experiencing as a result of being alone and separated from his companions. Regardless, Paul was so emotionally spent that he was fearful to the point of severe trembling (1 Cor. 2:3). (Note: The Greek word *tromos* comes from a root word that means dread or terrify. It is obvious that Paul was experiencing severe emotional trauma at the time he originally entered Corinth alone.)
b. Paul determined to trust only Jesus Christ and to make His glorious name known among the people of Corinth (1 Cor. 1:1-2). While this would have been a prime opportunity to resort to a Christianized version of Greek philosophy in an attempt to avoid the dangers of persecution, Paul refused to use secular methods in his personal interaction with the people or his public preaching of the gospel (1 Cor. 2:4). What a powerful testimony to His confidence in the Word and his willingness to remain true to his Savior!

13. 1. God gave Paul power to continue in spite of his weakened emotional condition.
    2. God brought two Christians named Aquila and Priscilla to Corinth at a time when Paul was separated from his missionary companions and desperately needed spiritual encouragement.
    3. Since they were also tentmakers like Paul, he stayed with them and worked with them (v. 3). This allowed the three of them to work together, and it gave Aquila and Priscilla additional time to encourage Paul during this difficult time in his life.
    4. Silas and Timothy, who had missed Paul at Athens, joined him in Corinth.
    5. The arrival of Timothy and Silas allowed Paul to devote himself completely to the Word (v. 5). Perhaps they worked to support Paul's full-time evangelistic efforts or they had brought a financial gift for Paul from the churches of Macedonia.

14. Paul was saying that he and the other apostolic representatives were no longer responsible for the presentation of the gospel to the Jews or for the ensuing divine judgment that they would experience as a result of their rejection of the truth. On the first missionary journey, Paul had understood the words of the prophet Isaiah to mean that God was directing Barnabas and him to begin evangelizing the Gentiles. Their ministry to the Gentiles was no longer to be accidental but intentional. However, they still did not believe that the priority of Jewish evangelism should be changed. In Acts 18, Paul is saying that the priority of Jewish evangelism would no longer apply. While Paul had previously gone first to the Jewish people in every city in which he ministered, he was now prepared to minister to anyone who would receive the message of salvation, regardless of ethnic background.

15. a. 1. Paul was able to stay at the home of Titius Justus, a man who worshipped God (v. 7). The text does not say why Paul did not continue to live with Aquila and Priscilla. Since they had been expelled from Rome under Emperor Claudius (cf. v. 2), their stay in Corinth was likely only temporary.
       2. Crispus, the leader of the synagogue, was saved along with his entire household (v. 8).
       3. Many of the Corinthians believed and were baptized (v. 8). God reassured Paul in a vision of His continuing presence and that he would not suffer physical harm during his stay in Corinth (vv. 9-10).
    b. Answers will vary.

16. The Jews wanted Gallio, the proconsul of Achaia, to classify the Christian and their beliefs as a non-authorized sect (vv. 13-14). (Note: The phrase "contrary to the law" refers to an illegal religious practice and a serious crime punishable by Roman law.) This would have brought the Christians living in the Roman province of Achaia under the direct judgment of the Roman state; however, Gallio refused to classify

the Christians and their beliefs as a separate religion and saw the Christian faith as a minor adaptation of the Jewish belief system (questions about words and names and your own law [cf. v. 15]). While Gallio's actions appear to be indifferent toward the plight of the believers, this is one example of how God used civil government to protect His people from serious harm.

Study #4a The Third Missionary Journey

1. When Apollos came to Ephesus and spoke in the synagogue, Aquila and Priscilla realized that his spiritual understanding was incomplete. They took him aside and explained to him the way of the Lord more accurately.

2. a. 1. Paul said that he planted the church, Apollos watered the church, but it is God who caused the growth (1 Cor. 3:6).
      2. Paul said he and Apollos were one, meaning that they were working together as a unit for God's glory (1 Cor. 3:8).
      3. Paul said that he and Apollos were God's fellow workers (1 Cor. 3:9).
   b. 1. The Corinthian believers were encouraged spiritually by Apollos' ministry (Acts 18:27). They were especially encouraged by the way he was able to refute the Jews in public (Acts 18:28).
      2. Unfortunately, many of the Corinthian Christians had the tendency to be followers of men rather than the Lord and some of them became rabid followers of Apollos rather than the Lord (1 Cor. 1:12).
   c. Answers will vary.

3. a. Paul attempted to find out if these disciples were NT believers who had been born again (Jn 3:5-8). Paul knew that anyone who had placed his faith in Christ alone for eternal life received the Holy Spirit. He also knew that anyone who did not have the Holy Spirit did not belong to Christ (Ro. 8:9).
   b. These individuals were disciples of John the Baptist. (Note: John taught genuine repentance toward God for the forgiveness of sins which was evidenced by good works and the willingness to be baptized [cf. Mk. 1:4].)
   c. These disciples were baptized in the name of the Lord Jesus (Acts 19:5). When Paul laid his hands on them, the Holy Spirit came upon them, and they spoke with tongues (i.e., the supernatural gift of being able to speak foreign languages without having learned them [cf. Acts 2:3-11]) and prophesied (Acts 19:6).

4. a. All those who lived in the Roman province of Asia heard the Word of the Lord, both Jews and Greeks.
   b. 1. Colossae (Col. 1:1-2). 2. Ephesus (Rev. 2:1). 3. Smyrna (Rev. 3:8). 4. Pergamum (Rev. 3:12). 5. Thyatira (Rev. 3:18). 6. Sardis (Rev. 4:1). 7. Philadelphia (Rev. 4:7). 8. Laodicea (Rev. 4:14).

5. a. 1. The evil spirit did not recognize the seven sons of Sceva (Acts 19:15). This is surprising since they were being used as instruments of Satan.
      2. The man who was possessed by the evil spirit leaped on them and subdued and overpowered them so that they fled out of the house naked and wounded (Acts 19:16).
   b. 1. Fear came upon all those who heard about these things (Acts 19:17).
      2. The name of the Lord Jesus was magnified (Acts 19:17).
      3. Many Christians who were engaged in evil practices (i.e., occult practices, etc.) confessed their sin and disclosed to others what they had been doing (Acts 19:18).
      4. Many people brought their magic art and evil books to a public site where they were burned in the sight of all (Acts 19:19).
      5. The Word of the Lord was growing mightily and prevailing (Acts 19:20).

6. a. God had used the preaching of the gospel to save several of the Ephesians. Many of these people had turned away from their idols and renounced their wicked ways. The salvation of the lost and the sanctification of those who had been saved adversely affected the business of selling miniature silver shrines (Acts 19:26). Paul had apparently been telling the people that the silver shrines were not gods (cf. Acts 19:26). Demetrius, one of the silversmiths, organized a meeting of the silversmiths who made the miniature silver shrines and told them that the business of selling sliver shrines was going to fall into disrepute (Acts 19:26). He also said that the temple of the great goddess Artemis would be regarded as worthless (i.e., the tourist trade would be destroyed [v. 27]). Demetrius' words enraged the other silversmiths and they began crying out, *"Great is Diana (i.e., Artemis) of the Ephesians."* Soon the entire city of Ephesus was filled with confusion and the mob dragged two of Paul's companions into the theater (Acts 19:29).
   b. Financial gain.

7. 1. He said that since Artemis is a god and all the people of Ephesus know this, she does not need to be defended against the attack of a few men (vv. 35-36).
   2. He said that those who had been accused had done nothing wrong (v. 37).
   3. He said that there was a proper legal procedure to follow through the Roman court. If a person violated the proper legal procedure, he might find himself in danger of being accused of starting a riot, which was a crime punishable by Roman law (vv. 38-40).

Study #4b   The Third Missionary Journey

8. The group appears to be made up of individuals from different levels of society. The name Aristarchus comes from the same Greek root as the English word aristocrat. Some commentators have suggested that Aristarchus was born of some degree of nobility while the other names in the group are much more common, perhaps indicating less noble parentage. (Note: The number of apostolic missionary helpers increases throughout the book of Acts from one on the first missionary journey [John Mark] to a sizable group of dedicated Christians who were willing to serve the Lord under the direction of Paul.)

9.
   1. God's people need to receive sound Biblical instruction from God-called Christian leaders so that they can do the work of the ministry (Eph. 4:11-12).
   2. They also need to be taught the Word of God so that they can develop the spiritual discernment they need to avoid false doctrine (Eph. 4:13-14).
   3. The need to be taught the Word of God so that they can learn how to speak the **"truth in love"** in order to edify other believers and evangelize the lost (Eph. 4:15). They need to join with other believers weekly to fulfill their Biblical responsibility of encouraging other believers (Heb. 10:24-25).

10. a. The various plots or attempts of the Jews to kill him. Notice that the text does not say *plot* but *plots*. The Jews planned various plots to kill Paul. Paul lived and ministered under the constant threat of death.
    b.
       1. Paul served the Lord with humility and sensitivity (Acts 2:19).
       2. Paul was spiritually courageous because he taught people the whole counsel of God (Acts 20:20, 27).
       3. He was a tireless worker for the Lord. He taught publicly (in the school of Tyrannus) and in the various house churches ("house to house" [Acts 20:20]). The second reference could also refer to a personal discipleship ministry that Paul carried on while he was in Ephesus. He also worked with his own hands to provide for his own needs and the needs of others (Acts 20:35).
       4. He was impartial in love for others, teaching both Jews and Greeks about their need for repentance (Acts 20:21).
       5. He was self-sacrificing (Acts 20:24). He said that he did not count his own life dear to himself so that he might finish the work that God had given him to do.
       6. He was not covetous of others' financial possessions (Acts 20:33).
       7. He was generous and helped support others (Acts 20:35).

11. a. The savage wolves were the false teachers who constantly prey upon God's people. The Bible pictures the church of God as a flock of sheep over which God has placed shepherds. The shepherds are called by God to feed and

protect His sheep. The savage wolves were those false teachers who attacked His sheep for their own personal gain. False teachers eventually came into the church at Ephesus when Timothy pastored the church (1 Tim. 1:6-7). (Note: In the Lord's parable of the Good Shepherd, the wolves are the false teachers who attempt to snatch the sheep [Jn 10:12]. Only those sheep that truly belong to the Good Shepherd are able to recognize His voice and follow Him [Jn. 10:27]. Jesus Christ is not only the Good Shepherd but also the Chief Shepherd who watches over His sheep to insure that His sheep are safe and adequately fed.)
   b. Paul said that men will rise up from within the church and speak perverse things. They will draw away some of the believers after them. (Note: One of the chief characteristics of a false teacher is his or her willingness to promote disharmony within the body of Christ by gathering a following within the church and then leading them out. It is interesting that disciples of Christ can be deceived so easily.)
   c. Paul said that he commended the Ephesian elders to God and to the word of His grace that was able to build them up and to give them the inheritance among those who are saved.

12. When Paul had finished speaking to the Ephesian elders at Miletus, he knelt down and prayed with them all (Acts 20:36). They began to weep aloud and embraced Paul and repeatedly kissed him (Acts 20:37). (Note: Kissing on the check is a middle-eastern expression of genuine love and affection.) They were especially grieved that they would not see his face again (Acts 20:37). They accompanied him to the ship (Acts 20:38).

13. a. Answers may vary but the answer should be "no." God has revealed all He is pleased to reveal about the future in His Word. God's people are warned not to add to the things written in the Book (cf. Rev. 22:18).
    b. One of the primary ministries of the Holy Spirit during this age is to guide man into all truth (i.e., the Word). When someone says that the Holy Spirit told him to do a certain thing, God's people should remember John 16:13, which says the Holy Spirit " **will not speak on His own authority."**

14. a. The residents of Ptolemais and Luke. Apparently Luke was not convinced until this time that Paul should not go to Jerusalem. The prophecy of Agabus must have convinced Luke of the wisdom of not going up to Jerusalem to deliver the financial gift to the brethren in Judea. Notice that Agabus did not say that Paul should not go to Jerusalem. He simply said that if he went, he would be bound and delivered into the hands of the Gentiles. His prophecy came true just as he had prophesied (cf. Acts 21:33).
    b. **"What do you mean by weeping and breaking my heart? For I am ready not only to be bound, but also to die at Jerusalem for the name of the Lord Jesus."**

c. God's will. This is an interesting passage because it shows that dedicated believers can disagree regarding God's will. Ultimately the each believer must make the final decision for himself, which others should accept as God's will for that individual's life. (Note: Christians who are less mature than the apostle Paul would be wise to consider seriously the spiritual counsel of other dedicated believers as Paul had earlier [cf. cf. Acts 16:10]. Apparently Paul was so convinced that this was God's will for his life that he was willing to reject the appeals of his friends to be faithful to God.)

Study #5a   Captured in Jerusalem

1. a. Paul emphasized the things that God did among the Gentiles through him. (Note: Unfortunately, it is easy for some Christians to emphasize what they have done for God with His help. The Bible says, **"He who glories, let him glory in the Lord"** [cf. 1 Cor. 1:31].)
    b. Answers will vary.

2. a. They were believing Jews who were zealous for the Law (Acts 21:20). They had a second-hand knowledge about Paul and his ministry and believed that Paul was teaching the Jews to forsake the Mosaic law (Acts 21:21).
    b. The Jewish elders wanted Paul to purify himself and to pay the necessary offerings of four poor Jewish Christians who had apparently taken a Nazirite vow (Acts 21:23). (Note: A Nazirite vow normally lasted for 30 days, after which the individual presented his hair as an offering and an appropriate sacrifice [cf. Nu. 6:14-18].) Paul's willingness to pay the offerings of these four individuals would have proved that he was not opposed to the Law.

3. No. Paul willingly complied with the elders' recommendation (Acts 21:26). Undoubtedly, Paul had a clear understanding of law and grace, and his willingness to comply with the elders' plan indicates that he believed that he could submit to their request without compromising his witness. (Note: Paul told the Corinthians that **"To the Jews I became as a Jew ..."** [1 Cor. 9:20]. To Paul this meant that he was willing to go as far as he could to reach the Jews for Christ as long as it did not violate Christ's commands. Again, to Paul, being a good Christian did not mean being a bad Jew.)

4. No. The legitimacy of man's actions must be based upon the objective revelation of God's Word rather than the subjective criteria of human experience. When a believer attempts to evaluate his own action or the actions of others by a subjective evaluation of human experience (i.e., cause and effect, etc.), he will soon lose sight of the authority of God's Word. While the law of "sowing and reaping" is certainly a Biblical principle (cf. Ga. 6:7-8), it is also true that man does not always reap immediate blessings from his obedience or immediate

repercussions as a result of his disobedience. If a believer does not understand this truth, he might be tempted to think that God endorses his sinful actions.

5. a. Answers will vary.
   b. A Christian should consider talking with those who are planning to baptize the child to explain his position. If the believer approached the potential hurtful situation with prayer and love, the friends or family will often be willing to listen to his perspective. The believer should explain that, as a Christian, his ultimate authority is the Word of God. He should also explain that "infant baptism" is not found in the Bible but is a man-made religious tradition that violates what the Biblical teaching of how to receive eternal life. He should also say that he wants to encourage those who desire to raise their children with a Christian influence but that his ultimate loyalty belongs to Christ. Perhaps, he could also give the other people the option of deciding whether they want him to attend, realizing that his presence should not be understood as an endorsement of the service. (Note: Some Christians are convicted that they should not attend a service of this nature. If they choose to do so, it is important that they communicate their reasons to others in a spirit of love.)

6. 1. In both situations the riots involved the whole cities (Acts 19:29; 21:30).
   2. In both situations the people rioting were not even sure what the problem was (Acts 19:32; 21:34).
   3. In both situations God used civil government to rescue the believers and preserve their lives (Acts 19:35-41; 21:32-33).

7. 1. Paul told the Roman soldiers that he was a Jew from Tarsus in Cilicia and a Roman citizen (Acts 21:39). They previously thought that he was an Egyptian rebel (cf. Acts 21:38).
   2. He raised his hand to the Jews and addressed them in the Hebrew dialect (Acts 21:40).

8. a. 3-5.
   b. 6-10.
   c. 11-21.

Study #5b Captured in Jerusalem

9. a. **"For I will send you far from here to the Gentiles"** (Acts 22:21).
   b. The people began to shout, throw off their cloaks and toss dust into the air (Acts 22:22-23). Lysias, the Roman commander (cf. Acts 24:7), heard about the disturbance and sent soldiers to arrest Paul and bring him into the

barracks (i.e., the Antonio Fortress) where they planned to examine him by scourging. When they tied Paul with thongs, he said, **"Is it lawful for you to scourge a man who is a Roman?"** The Roman soldiers were surprised at his citizenship and immediately told Lysias about Paul's true identity.

10. a. Paul meant that he did not allow the failures of the past (including his sins) to negatively affect the present. (Note: The only way that any individual is able to do this is to understand and accept the forgiveness that only Christ can offer. Paul was able to accept Christ's full forgiveness for his own sins because Paul acted ignorantly in unbelief [cf. 1 Tim. 1:13].)
    b. A Christian should trust God's Word rather than his feelings. Often a Christian who says that he cannot forgive himself is trying to do a form of spiritual penance because he is overcome with grief over his sin. However, he needs to realize that not accepting God's promise of complete forgiveness is also sin, which will keep him from fulfilling God's plan for his life. While a believer might appear humble as he wallows in self-disparagement over his past sin, it is really his pride that is encouraging him not to accept God's Word.
    c. Answers will vary. **"If we confess our sins, He is faithful and just to forgive us our sins and to cleanse us from all unrighteousness."**
    d. 1. He should trust God rather than his feelings. 2. He should seek godly counsel if he is unable to overcome the spiritual problem. 3. He should seek to make restitution if possible. (Note: An unwillingness to make restitution is a major reason why some believers do not experience God's assurance of forgiveness.) 4. He should examine his own heart to see whether he fully understands repentance (cf. 2 Cor. 7:9-11). Other answers could apply.

11. Paul said, **"God will strike you, you whitewashed wall! For you sit to judge me according to the law, and do you command me to be struck contrary to the law?"** (Acts 23:3). (Note: Paul's comment was as much prophetic as it was retaliatory. In the last days of Ananias' life, he was hunted down and killed by his own people.)

12. Some Bible commentators have interpreted Paul's failure in this situation to be the result of poor eyesight (cf. Ga. 4:15). However, it is also possible that the high priest was not wearing any priestly robes and Paul did not know that he was the high priest. Regardless, Paul was willing to "salute the uniform" even if he could not respect the man.

13. a. 1. Weak (1 Cor. 8:7). 2. Good (1 Tim. 1:5). 3. Pure (1 Tim. 3:9). 4. Seared (1 Tim. 4:2). 5. Defiled (Ti. 1:15).
    b. Religious good works are unable to make a worshipper perfect.

14. a. The blood of Christ (i.e., salvation). b. Answers will vary.

15. The NT Sadducees could be compared to any number of religious groups that deny the reality of eternity. Religious liberals (i.e, members of the National and World Council of Churches) are similar in many of the religious views to the Sadducees. Other answers could apply.

16. a. Forty Jews formed a conspiracy under oath and asked the Jewish leaders to petition the Roman commander for an opportunity to examine Paul. If Lysias was willing to allow Paul to be interrogated by the Jewish leaders, the forty Jews planned to assassinate him as he was being brought to the Jewish inquiry (Acts 23:15).
    b. God allowed Paul's nephew to overhear about the assassination plot (Acts 23:16). Paul's nephew told Paul of the plot (Acts 23:16). Paul instructed one of the Roman soldiers to take his nephew to the commander (Acts 23:17-18). After hearing the report, the commander told Paul's nephew not to tell anyone about the assassination attempt (Acts 23:21-22).

Study #6a   Imprisoned at Caeserea

1. Claudius Lysias called two of his centurions and ordered them to organize two hundred soldiers, seventy horsemen, and two hundred spearmen and escort Paul to Caesarea (Acts 23:23). He also wrote a letter to Felix, the governor of Judea, explaining the situation (Acts 23:25-30).

2. 1. Felix said that he would give Paul a hearing after his accusers arrived.
   2. He gave his soldiers orders to place Paul in Herod's Praetorium. (Note: Herod the Great built a summer palace at Caesarea which later served as the governor's headquarters and a prison.)

3. a. 1. He said Paul was a pest (v. 5). 2. He said Paul was a fellow who stirs up dissension among all the Jews throughout the world (v. 5). 3. He said Paul was a ringleader of the sect of the Nazarenes (v. 5). 4. He said Paul tried to desecrate the temple (v. 6). (Note: Tertullus made the situation look as if the Jews had protected the temple from desecration and prevented a major social disturbance even though the opposite was quite true.)

    b. Tertullus said that Claudius Lysias used much violence when he took Paul out of their hands. (Note: Notice that Tertullus impugns the actions of Claudius Lysias without saying categorically that he was in error. Had Felix quickly come to the Roman Commander's defense, Tertullus could have easily explained that he did not mean Claudius Lysias had done anything wrong.

4. a. Felix reserved judgment until hearing Paul's side of the story. He allowed Paul to present his side of the story without restricting him in any way or even questioning him, which would assume wrongdoing on Paul's part.
   b. A believer should remember that there are two sides to every story. He should also be aware of the temptation to believe the first person's story and to regard the second story with skepticism.
   c. It is a shame and a folly to him.

5. a. Tertullus appears to flatter Felix while Paul simply addressed him in a respectful manner.
   b. 1. Flattery can be used by ungodly people to entice and seduce the opposite sex (Pro. 7:21).
      2. Flattery causes ruin or destruction (e.g., mistrust, etc. [Prov. 26:28]).
      3. Flattery can be used by anyone to deceive innocent, trusting followers (Ro. 16:18).
      4. Flattery can be used to gain an advantage over other people (Ju. 16).

6. a. 1. A person needs his conscience cleansed by the blood of Jesus Christ by being born again (Heb. 9:11-14).
      2. A believer needs to confess his sins so that his fellowship with God is not adversely affected by the haunting of a guilty conscience.
   b. 1. A believer needs to make sure that no other person has an offense against him that he cannot solve (Matt. 5:23-24). If the believer is aware that another person has something against him, he should go to that person and attempt to resolve the problem, even if the other person is the offender or appears unwilling to offer forgiveness.
      2. A believer should not retaliate when another person does wrong (Ro. 12:17). If a believer retaliates, he will receive a guilty conscience for his sin and have to humble himself and confess his sin to the one who hurt him in the first place; this is not an easy thing to do.
      3. A believer should do everything he can to live at peace with all men (Ro. 12:18). This does not mean that a believer can live at peace with all men (e.g., Jesus Christ, Paul, Peter, John, etc.). The verse means that the believer must make sure that he does everything he can to live in harmony with other people. His actions should never lead to sin in order to make peace with others.

7. 1. Felix put them off by saying, **"When Lysias the commander comes down, I will make a decision on your case"** (Acts 24:22).

2. He ordered Paul to be kept in prison, but he gave him some freedom and allowed his friends to minister to him (Acts 24:23). (Note: It appears that Felix believed that Paul was innocent since he gave him so much freedom. His willingness to keep Paul in prison might have been an attempt to appease the Jews and prevent a public disturbance in Jerusalem.)

8. a. Felix became frightened and said, **"Go away for now; when I have a convenient time I will call for you."** (Note: The Greek word for frightened [*emphobos* - frightened, terrified, cf. phobia] indicates that Felix experienced extreme fear.) Like Felix, some people want to hear about what it means to have faith in Christ, but often they do not want to hear about how it will affect their lives. With the help of a Cypriot magician named Atomos, Felix persuaded Drusilla to leave her husband at the age of sixteen. Accordingly, she joined him as his third wife, hardly a righteous act of self-control that would escape the judgment of God. Drusilla bore Felix one son named Agrippa who met his death in the eruption of Vesuvius in 79 A. D.
   b. Felix hoped that Paul would give him money (Acts 24:26). Apparently Felix thought that either Paul had some money or that his steady supply of visitors (cf. Acts 24:23) could easily acquire it for him. (Note: Paul's refusal to buy his freedom reflects his willingness to remain in the place of God's choosing rather than trying to better his personal situation.) If God's people can learn to become content where He has placed them (even in prison), they will find that He will give them peace and use them greatly for His glory.
   c. Answers will vary but could include: 1. They actually believe that they are saved even though they have never trusted Christ alone for eternal life. 2. They like to be around religious and moral people who provide a positive influence on their lives. 3. They believe they can somehow earn favor with God even though they are probably hearing messages of salvation by grace through faith alone. 4. They attend churches that teach good works will save them.

Study #6b   Imprisoned at Caeserea

9. a. Festus asked Paul to stand trial in Jerusalem in order to appease the Jews. This wicked action had nothing to do with justice. When Paul appealed to be tried before a Roman court (i.e., Caesar), Festus said that he would be sent to Rome to stand trial even though he had no substantial charges to bring against him (cf. Acts 25:26).
   b. The unsaved nations and their leaders reject God's laws and killed Jesus Christ (i.e., His Anointed) in an attempt to overthrow God's sovereign rule over this world (Ps. 2:1-2). The unsaved devise plans (and institute laws) that are designed to unshackle themselves and society from any vestiges of God's moral law (e.g., legalized abortion, homosexuality, etc. [Ps. 2:3]). However,

God laughs at their feeble attempts and terrifies them in His anger (Ps. 2:5).

10. a. Festus said that the charges against Paul were simply some points of disagreement about the Jewish religion and about a certain dead man named Jesus whom Paul said was alive.
    b. Festus was utterly lost. He thought Jesus was a dead man.

11. 1. Part one (vv. 2-11). 2. Part two (vv. 12-18). 3. Part three (vv. 19-23).

12. a. Answers will vary.
    b. Answers will vary.
    c. Answers will vary.

13. a. Paul was saying that he had obeyed all that God had originally revealed to him on the road to Damascus when he was saved. This included being a witness to the Jews and the Gentiles and attempting to turn their hearts from the darkness to the light of God (i.e., salvation).
    b. Answers will vary.
    c. Answers will vary but should include: 1. Be sure that you are saved. 2. Pray for wisdom and study the Scriptures. 3. Dedicate yourself to God as a living sacrifice (cf. Ro. 12:1-2). 3. Live a holy life before God and others.

14. a. 1. Festus thought Paul was out of his mind (Acts 26:24).
       2. Agrippa was almost persuaded to be saved (Acts 26:28).
    b. 1. Paul assured Festus that he was not crazy and the things that he was telling him were words of sober truth (Acts 26:25).
       2. Paul called upon Agrippa as a witness of the things that he was saying (Acts 26:26).
       3. Paul turned his evangelistic attention to Agrippa who had been silent up until this time (Acts 26:27). Perhaps Paul assumed that Festus' unwillingness to accept his explanation was evidence of his lack of openness.

15. Answers will vary.

Study #7a   The Journey to Rome

1. Luke ("we") and Aristarchus. (Note: Throughout the book of Acts the "we" sections [cf. Acts 16:10-16; 20:5-16; 27:1-28:16] indicate that Luke, the writer of Acts, periodically joined Paul on his missionary journeys.)

Leader's Guide 73

2. a. 1. God motivated Roman commander Julius to treat Paul with consideration and to allow him to go to his friends and receive care (Acts 27:3).
      2. God allowed Luke, a physician, to travel with Paul who apparently needed some care (Acts 27:3; cf. Col. 4:14).
   b. Answers will vary.

3. No. God had already told Paul that he wanted him to go to Rome. God's people should never allow adversity to cause them to doubt the clear teaching of Scripture.

4. a. 1. God's people experience adversity because they live in a fallen world (Jn. 16:33).
      2. God's people experience adversity as a result of their own sin. God does not always exempt His people from the law of sowing and reaping (Gal. 6:7).
      3. God's people experience adversity because they are the special target of satanic attack (Eph. 6:11-12).
      4. God's people experience adversity in the form of God's discipline so that they might become partakers of His holiness (Heb. 12:5-10).
      5. God's people experience adversity so that they might learn to rejoice in their future exaltation (1 Pet. 4:12-13).
   b. 1. A Christian should ask God in prayer to reveal sin in his life (Ps. 139:23).
      2. He should also search the Scriptures to learn what God expects from him. (Note: If a Christian prays sincerely and asks God to reveal sin in his life, he can trust God to answer his prayer. If he is also studying the Word, he can trust God to reveal to him any sin in his life that might result in God's chastisement. If God does not reveal anything to him, the believer should assume that the present difficulties that he is facing are a trial of faith and rejoice that God has considered him worthy to endure the trial, trusting God to use him as a testimony of His grace.

5. a. 1. The harbor at Fair Havens was not suitable to winter the ship (Acts 27:12).
      2. The harbor at Phoenix was a more suitable place to winter the ship because it faced southwest and northwest (Acts 27:12).
      3. A moderate south wind came up that made them think that they could make it to Phoenix (Acts 27:13). This kind of wind was unusual for that time of the year.
   b. Shortly after their departure, a violent wind known as a Euraquilo (i.e., a northeaster) came up and drove the ship off course and away from the island (Acts 27:15). Over the next several days, the ship and its passengers were driven along by the sea until they had lost all hope of being saved (Acts 27:15-20).

c. "Men, you should have listened to me, and not have sailed from Crete and incurred this disaster and loss."

6. 1. Paul told the people that they should have followed his advice, not because of who he was, but because of what God had told him (Acts 27:21-23). Paul was confident that what God had told him was true and he reminded the people that they were not rejecting his counsel, but God's Word.
   2. It is also likely that he was preparing them to be more open-minded to his counsel in the future (Acts 27:31-32).

7. It appears that Paul prayed for the safety and preservation of everyone (not just some) on the ship. God told Paul that He would grant (a response to a request) him all those who were sailing with him. (Note: If Paul did ask God for the preservation of everyone's life as it appears, it is evidence of great faith since both the circumstances appeared impossible and the passengers, including Luke, (cf. Acts 27:20) had lost hope. Sometimes all it takes is one person who is willing to trust God in the midst of an impossible situation to see God grant a victory.

8. 1. God allowed them to see a certain bay with a beach even though they did not know where they were (Acts 27:39).
   2. God allowed enough wind to drive the ship on to the beach (Acts 27:40).
   3. God enabled the sailors to direct the ship to the exact location they had wanted (Acts 27:41).
   4. God allowed the ship to break up enough so that those who could not swim had something to hold on to help them float to shore (Acts 27:44).
   5. God allowed everyone to get to shore safely (Acts 27:44).

Study #7b   The Journey to Rome

9. a. A viper came out of the fire and attached itself to Paul's hand (Acts 28:3).
   b. The islanders changed their minds and thought he was a god (Acts 28:6).

10. a. His own mind. (Note: When a Christian employs this method of determining truth, he is engaged in a form of humanism even if he does not realize it.)
    b. 1. Mysticism leads the believer away from the authority of God and His Word.
       2. The believer has no objective way to ascertain the truth.
       3. The believer often becomes preoccupied with the physical circumstances around him rather than focusing on Jesus Christ. Other answers could apply.

Leader's Guide 75

11. a. Paul was allowed to stay by himself with a soldier guarding him (Acts 28:16). He called the leading Jews of the area and told them why he had been imprisoned without cause (Acts 28:17-20). The Jews responded by saying that they had not received any formal charges against Paul, nor did they know anything bad about him (Acts 28:21). They also said they wanted to hear his views for themselves since they had heard negative reports about the "sect" to which Paul belonged (Acts 28:22).
    b. Paul arranged for a time to speak to all the leading Jews at Rome (Acts 28:23). The Jews came in large numbers, and he explained to them the kingdom of God and he tried to persuade them to be saved by using the Law of Moses and the prophets (Acts 28:23). He spoke to them from morning to evening (Acts 28:23).
    c. Some of the Jews were persuaded (i.e., they were saved), but others would not believe (Acts 28:24).

12. Paul spoke one parting word to those who would not believe (Acts 28:24). He quoted from the prophet Isaiah (Is. 6:9-10), who foretold of Israel's rejection of the truth. Paul also quoted the psalmist (Ps. 98:3) to tell the Jews that the message of salvation would be accepted by the Gentiles (Acts 28:28).

13. a. Answers will vary.
    b. Answers will vary.